The Collected Hymns of
CARL P. DAW, JR.

A YEAR
OF
GRACE

HYMNS for the
CHURCH YEAR

Code No. 935

Hope Publishing Company
CAROL STREAM IL 60188

FOREWORD

1990 is a year of special significance for those who write hymns and the millions who sing hymns here in the United States. The first book ever printed in English-speaking North America was published in Cambridge, Massachusetts, exactly three hundred and fifty years ago. When it appeared in 1640, *The Whole Booke of Psalmes faithfully translated into English metre* was quickly adopted by almost all the congregations in the Massachusetts Bay Colony. In his preface to *The Bay Psalm Book*, as it soon became known, Richard Mather wrote of its intended purpose in these words:

> "....that soe we may sing in Sion the Lord's songs
> of praise according to his own will; until he take us
> from hence, and wipe away all our tears, and bid us
> enter our masters joy to sing eternal Hallelujahs".

The purpose of writing and singing hymns has not changed in three and a half centuries, though clearly the accepted spelling of English has! And, along with the spelling, the repertoire of hymns has changed. The range of occasions and topics which any collection of hymns now addresses has widened, and this is only to be expected in light of that celebrated couplet written in 1845 by James Russell Lowell:

> "New occasions teach new duties,
> time makes ancient good uncouth."

New encounters with God require fresh songs of praise, and time renders many an old hymn unattractive to later generations. And so, like the glad work of hymn-singing, the good work of hymn-writing continues century after century to the glory of God and the upbuilding of God's people.

In that spirit Carl Daw has written this collection of sixty-six hymns for the Church Year. They express the saving truths of the Gospel in powerful contemporary language, and they speak to new liturgical needs on the part of Christian congregations at worship. Here are paraphrases of the biblical canticles to be sung in grateful response to God's Word in the Old and New Testament alike; here are songs of praise to center our attention on God's grace mediated to us in baptism and Eucharist; here are texts meant to give new life to some of the noblest of tunes, among them *Jerusalem*, *Russia* and *Thaxted*; here are additional stanzas cunningly crafted to fit the language of an earlier period in the life of the Church.

In this collection the great themes of the Church Year are set forth in new and striking ways. Among other things, this will help to rescue the agony of Good Friday and the great promise of Pentecost from the familiarity which breeds an all too easy acceptance of the mystery of God at work for our salvation:

"The language which we knew so well
flowed smoothly on the tongue,
though seldom did we pause to weigh
how things were said or sung.
But now the world is showing us
with stunning clarity
the problems with the words we used
to tame a mystery".

("O God, on whom we lost our hold")

Already some of these texts are part of the hymn repertoire in a variety of denominational settings. "Christ the Victorious" has its place at funerals, "Like the murmur. of the dove's song" is being sung at ordinations and confirmation services, and "O day of peace that dimly shines" is on people's lips when they gather to pray for justice and peace in our troubled world. And other texts to be found here will win that same wide acceptance. "Into Jerusalem Jesus rode" will be sung on Palm Sunday, "Sing of Andrew, John's disciple" will be on our lips in the Decade of Evangelism with people of other faiths and none living not across the world now but across the street, and "The house of faith has many rooms" will speak to the present pace of invention and the present scope of critical enquiry which far outstrip what previous generations have known:

"We dare not limit God's domain
to what our creeds declare,
or shrink from probing things unknown
lest God should not be there".

("The house of faith has many rooms")

So three hundred and fifty years after the publication of *The Bay Psalm Book*, and on the eve of the third Christian millennium, here are new hymns to sing throughout the Church Year. Like the seventeenth-century Puritans in New England who sang on their uncertain journey across an ill-mapped and unfamiliar landscape, we need words to express our hopes and fears and to celebrate our faith and fellowship along the road to God's future. For addressing this need we can be thankful to Carl Daw who speaks for us all when he writes:

"So we dare to journey on,
led by faith through ways untrod,
till we come at last like John
to behold the Lamb of God"

("Wild and lone the prophet's voice")

Jeffery W. Rowthorn
Bishop Suffragan
Episcopal Diocese of
Connecticut

To May and Elizabeth,
who have had faith

INTRODUCTION

The texts collected in this volume represent my first nine years of hymnwriting. In many ways they are more notable for their differences from each other than for their sameness. Although the texts are loosely grouped according to liturgical season or topical affinity, each section contains texts of various styles and origins. A number of them, for example, are paraphrases of scripture, and others are translations of Latin or German hymns. In texts derived from such sources, I have usually felt a responsibility to maintain the tone and content of the original version as much as possible and have generally resisted the urge to do something different. Comparable restraints have also shaped texts written for specific tunes or for a certain occasion or for a particular parish. But I dare to hope that the special circumstances of each text's composition (usually mentioned in the notes on the facing page), while welcome, will not prevent these hymns from voicing effectively a more general expression of human aspiration and faith.

Something also needs to be said about the language of these texts. A number of my earlier texts have been revised for this collection, but some of them (especially previously-published ones) retain masculine nouns and pronouns for God. This inherited and traditional idiom conveys a sense of divine personality more effectively than any genderless approach can, yet it runs the great risk of seeming to limit God to male/patriarchal images. Although the early warnings of the inadequacy of such language came primarily from women who felt excluded, the problem of God-language cannot be solved by substituting feminine language for masculine language. The issue, rather, is how to transcend the limitations of human gender when talking about God. The challenge of doing so is especially acute in poetry, because the economy of poetic diction does not permit the wordy circumlocutions possible in the more elastic patterns of prose. On the other hand, the constraints of poetry have the virtue of encouraging more creative use of direct address (You), relative pronouns (who/whom/whose), and indefinite passive constructions implying God's activity.

There are comparable problems with other received religious imagery. For example, the idea that God is *above* us may have made sense when the earth was thought to be flat and to hover in the middle of a three-tiered universe. In our day, we can more responsibly and effectively communicate the intended meaning of such phrases by speaking of a boundless God or a God who is beyond our human comprehension. It is imperative that we honor the intention rather than simply the language of the Judeo-Christian heritage.

Such a hermeneutical concern is one of the reasons this collection contains metrical paraphrases of all the canticles, invitatories, and appointed hymns from the Daily Office of the Book of Common Prayer 1979.[1] These are not intended to replace the Prayer Book versions but to enhance awareness of their essence, so that the Prayer Book canticles can be used with greater appreciation and understanding. Also, many of these paraphrases have been provided in ungendered forms to mitigate the unrelieved masculine language of the Prayer Book. Because these are, after all, scriptural texts, their usefulness is by no means limited to these particular liturgical occasions. Indeed, one of my hopes is that some of these paraphrases will make available to the broader Christian community the riches of scriptural hymnody which have been treasured by many generations of worshipers in the liturgical churches.

To present these texts without music has the advantage of calling attention to their form and content as Christian verse, but it also deprives them of some of their real strength. Especially in the case of texts written for specific tunes, there is intended to be a melding of words and music to yield a unified expression of praise or prayer. This is not a book meant for reading but for singing—or at the very least, for humming! Even the scansion of some texts will seem strange until they are heard with their proper tunes. Yet I also hope that these texts will continue to evoke new tunes, as some of them have already done, because such new settings often expand and enhance the original intention of the words.[2]

In the course of writing these texts I have received many kindnesses for which I am grateful. To my colleagues on the Text Committee for *The Hymnal 1982*, and especially to the Rev. Dr. Marion J. Hatchett who chaired it, I am indebted for their patience and encouragement as I made my first efforts at hymnwriting. Their suggestions greatly improved my work then, and the principles they articulated have continued to help me evaluate and polish what I write.

The first part of this collection has gradually taken shape in response to the urging of Alec Wyton to attempt (as he put it) "a new Keble"—i.e. a series of texts comparable to Keble's *Christian Year*. I am thankful for his suggestion and hope this beginning offers something of what he envisioned. Significant portions of this plan have been undertaken as commissioned texts, and I have indicated in the notes for each text where this has been the case. I deeply appreciate all those who provided the opportunities to write these texts.

More than a third of these texts took shape during my sabbatical in the summer of 1989. I am profoundly grateful to the people of St. Mark's Chapel in Storrs, Connecticut, for enabling me to have this time away from the parish (and for their ongoing good-naturedness in allowing me to try out many of these texts in the context of worship). The hospitality of the Society of St. John the Evangelist in Cambridge, Massachusetts, at the beginning of this period provided an ideal environment for embarking on the final stages of this project, and Brian Wren's flat in England allowed me the solitude needed to complete the writing. I am most thankful for both these havens.

Throughout the years of writing these texts, I have benefited from the advice and encouragement of many friends. I hesitate to name particular persons in addition to those already mentioned, lest I offend by omission; but I would be remiss not to acknowledge the invaluable help of Elizabeth M. Downie, Raymond F. Glover, Michael W. Merriman, and David Ashley White. Nor can I imagine working with a more considerate and cooperative publisher than George Shorney.

To my immediate family, my wife May and our daughter Elizabeth, I am grateful beyond telling for many years of patient support, quiet confidence, and judicious criticism. They have gracefully endured the vagaries of hymnwriting created both by my presence and by my absence, and it is a great pleasure to dedicate this book to them.

Storrs, Connecticut
January 1990

1. All page references to the Book of Common Prayer are to this edition.

2. It is hoped that editions of these texts with music will be forthcoming. Composers who wish to have settings for these texts considered for future publications are encouraged to submit them to the publisher.

CONTENTS

II. HYMNS FOR THE PEOPLE OF GOD

THE MYSTERY OF GOD

THE CHURCH'S PRAISE

CHRISTIAN MINISTRY

THE LIFE OF FAITH

HYMNS FOR DAILY LIFE

FROM WORSHIP TO WITNESS

ADVENT

✛

This text was written for an Advent hymn competition sponsored by the Hymn Society of America in 1985.

TUNE: For the hymn competition David Ashley White composed the tune EXPECTATION for this text. Of the published tunes, BLAENHAFREN, TON-Y-BOTEL, and NETTLETON seem to work best. The unusual rhyme scheme here, which links the first and last rhymes of each stanza (then repeats the last rhyme word as the first of the succeeding stanza), needs to be imitated in the musical structure of the tune.

1 Because "advent" means "coming," each stanza of this hymn focuses on a different aspect of Christ's coming to humanity in the past, the present, and the future and on various groups of people who anticipate or experience it. The first stanza concerns the expectations attending Israel's hope for the coming of the Messiah.

2 Stanza two deals with Christ's present coming to Christians through scripture, prayer, and sacraments.

3 The final stanza celebrates Christ's coming in power and great glory to reign over all the world (cf. Revelation 12:14-19). The penultimate line is an allusion to Psalm 85:10.

FOR THE COMING OF THE SAVIOR

8 7. 8 7. D

1 For the coming of the Savior
    who would reign on David's throne,
free God's people from oppression,
    and restore their heritage;
Israel looked with expectation
    for the dawning of that age,
and we share their sense of longing:
    in their hope, we see our own.

2 By the coming of the Savior
    who is present with his own
in the sacraments and scripture,
    and the bidden calm of prayer;
Christians still this truth discover
    and a timeless blessing share
greater than sheer thought can fathom:
    for by faith is Christ made known.

3 At the coming of the Savior
    who in splendor will be known
when he vanquishes Death's legions,
    and returns to reign in might;
all the world at last shall witness
    how God's judgment can unite
truth with mercy, peace with justice:
    joined in love through Christ alone.

—Carl P. Daw, Jr.

This translation of a hymn by Philip Nicolai was prepared for *The Hymnal 1982.* Nicolai was the pastor in Unna, Westphalia, where a terrible epidemic raged from July 1597 to January 1598. During that time, more than 1300 people perished, and Nicolai's parsonage overlooked the churchyard where the daily interments often numbered as many as thirty. This text was published in an appendix to a book of meditations he wrote during those months when he was much occupied with thoughts of the life to come.

TUNE: This text is intended to be sung to its proper tune WACHET AUF.

1 "Sleepers, wake!" is used here for the stronger German opening (literally, "Wake up!") because that has become the standard way of identifying this text in English. Although the present translation occasionally incorporates lines from earlier English versions, it tries to convey more of the vigor and narrative urgency of the German original. The first stanza alludes to the parable of the Wise and Foolish Maidens (Matthew 25:1-13).

2 This stanza includes echoes of Ezekiel 8:17 and Revelation 19:6-9.

3 The vision of the heavenly Jerusalem includes material from Revelation 21:21 and probably reflects Nicolai's reading in Augustine's *City of God* during this time.

"SLEEPERS, WAKE!"
A VOICE ASTOUNDS US

89.8.89.8.66.4.88

1 "Sleepers, wake!" A voice astounds us,
   the shout of rampart-guards surrounds us:
     "Awake, Jerusalem, arise!"
   Midnight's peace their cry has broken,
   their urgent summons clearly spoken:
     "The time has come, O maidens wise!
       Rise up, and give us light;
       the Bridegroom is in sight.
        Alleluia!
   Your lamps prepare and hasten there,
   that you the wedding feast may share."

2 Zion hears the watchmen singing;
   her heart with joyful hope is springing,
     she wakes and hurries through the night.
   Forth he comes, her Bridegroom glorious
   in strength of grace, in truth victorious:
     her star is risen, her light grows bright.
       Now come, most worthy Lord,
       God's Son, Incarnate Word,
        Alleluia!
   We follow all and heed your call
   to come into the banquet hall.

3 Lamb of God, the heavens adore you;
   let saints and angels sing before you,
     as harps and cymbals swell the sound.
   Twelve great pearls, the city's portals:
   through them we stream to join th' immortals
     as we with joy your throne surround.
       No eye has known the sight,
       no ear heard such delight:
        Alleluia!
   Therefore we sing to greet our King;
   for ever let our praises ring.

            —Philipp Nicolai;
              trans. Carl P. Daw, Jr.

The text was written for an Advent hymn competition sponsored by the Hymn Society of America in 1985. It is a paraphrase of Canticle 4/16: The Song of Zechariah or *Benedictus Dominus Deus* (BCP, pp. 50-51, 92-93) from Luke 1:68-79.

TUNE: For the hymn competition, this text was submitted with David Ashley White's tune ZECHARIAH It can also be sung effectively to KINGSFOLD or FOREST GREEN.

1 Because this canticle represents Zechariah's ecstatic outburst—after nine months of silence—at the circumcision of his son John (Luke 1:20-22, 63-64), the language is kept deliberately simple. Because John the Baptist figures so prominently in the Advent readings, this hymn is especially appropriate for that season. The addition of Davidic branch and tree imagery here is based on Isaiah 11:1,10 and Revelation 5:5.

2 This stanza emphasizes God's covenantal faithfulness (*hesed*) and echoes numerous passages from Hebrew scripture (e.g. Psalm 105:8, 106:45: Micah 7:20; Genesis 22:16-17, 26:3; Jeremiah 11:5). Although Zechariah is a priest, the worship he describes involves not simply cultic activity but the whole life of God's people.

3 Here the general hymn of praise yields to a specific blessing on the newborn child, incorporating language from Malachi 3:1 and Isaiah 40:3. John is seen as the herald of a new age in which God's past promises will be brought to fulfillment.

Blessed Be the God of Israel

CMD

1 Blessed be the God of Israel
   who comes to set us free
and raises up new hope for us:
   a Branch from David's tree.
So have the prophets long declared
   that with a mighty arm
God would turn back our enemies
   and all who wish us harm.

2 With promised mercy will God still
   the covenant recall,
the oath once sworn to Abraham,
   from foes to save us all;
that we might worship without fear
   and offer lives of praise,
in holiness and righteousness
   to serve God all our days.

3 My child, as prophet of the Lord
   you will prepare the way,
to tell God's people they are saved
   from sin's eternal sway.
Then shall God's mercy from on high
   shine forth and never cease
to drive away the gloom of death
   and lead us into peace.

—Carl P. Daw, Jr.

This text was written for a Hymn Society of America competition for Advent Hymns in 1985.

TUNE: This hymn was submitted to the competition with David Ashley White's tune JOSEPHINE. It can also be sung effectively to ABERYSTWYTH.

1 All four gospels identify John the Baptist with the prophecy of Isaiah 40:3 (see Matthew 3:1-12, Mark 1:2-8; Luke 3:1-20: John 1:19-28). The preaching attributed to him in stanzas 1 and 2 is based primarily on the account in Matthew.

2 There are intentional echoes here of Galatians 5:22-23 and Colossians 3:1-2.

3 The final stanza attempts to blend the acclamation of John the Baptist (John 1:29,36) with the frequent images of the triumphant Lamb in the Book of Revelation (5:6-14). See also the hymns, "Mark how the Lamb of God's self-offering" (p. 45), "God's Paschal Lamb is sacrificed for us" (p.75), and "Splendor and honor, majesty and power" (p. 115).

WILD AND LONE THE PROPHET'S VOICE

7.7.7.7.D

1 Wild and lone the prophet's voice
    echoes through the desert still,
calling us to make a choice,
    bidding us to do God's will:
"Turn from sin and be baptized;
    cleanse your heart and mind and soul.
Quitting all the sins you prized,
    yield your life to God's control."

2 "Bear the fruit repentance sows:
    lives of justice, truth, and love.
Trust no other claim than those;
    set your heart on things above.
Soon the Lord will come in power,
    burning clean the threshing floor:
then will flames the chaff devour;
    wheat alone shall fill God's store."

3 With such preaching stark and bold
    John proclaimed salvation near,
and his timeless warnings hold
    words of hope to all who hear.
So we dare to journey on,
    led by faith through ways untrod,
till we come at last like John
    to behold the Lamb of God.

—Carl P. Daw, Jr.

This text was written in 1985 for an Advent Hymn Contest sponsored by the Hymn Society of America.

TUNE: For the contest mentioned above, David Ashley White wrote the tune KINGDOM OF LOVE. No published tune is known in this metre.

1 The first stanza paraphrases Isaiah 40:3-4; 35:1-2,5-6.

2 The second stanza is based on Zephaniah 3:14-20.

3 The third stanza blends images from Psalm 72:1-7, Isaiah 11:6-9, and Micah 4:1-4.

MAKE STRAIGHT IN THE DESERT A HIGHWAY

97.98.98.98

1 Make straight in the desert a highway,
   prepare the way of the Lord:
       let mountains and hills bow down humbly
       and valleys rise up for their King.
   In joy shall the wilderness blossom,
   and streams through the desert be poured:
       the eyes of the blind shall be opened,
       and tongues that were silent shall sing.

2 Break forth into singing, O Zion,
   your King is coming to you.
       Jerusalem, shout with rejoicing,
       he comes to redeem you from fear.
   For God shall bring peace and abundance,
   your praise and renown to renew:
       prepare to receive your salvation:
       the promised Redeemer is near.

3 The reign of the Lord will be gracious,
   its blessings ever will last;
       for then will God bring to fulfillment
       the promise of peace from above.
   All creatures will prosper together,
   to plowshares all swords will be cast:
       earth's people will find their true freedom
       in God's perfect kingdom of Love.

—Carl P. Daw, Jr.

TUNE: This text was written for use with the tune NUN KOMM DER HEIDEN HEILAND.

1 The imagery here is drawn from Revelation 22:16 (based on Numbers 24:17) and Isaiah 9:2. The recurring attention to Jesus as the Word derives from the Prologue to John's gospel (1:1-18).

2 This stanza emphasizes the coming of Jesus in history through his incarnation, with reference to the birth narratives of Matthew (1:18-2:23) and Luke (1:26-2:40) and with allusion to the Passion narratives of all four gospels phrased in overtones of Isaiah 53:3-5.

3 The third stanza evokes the present coming of Jesus to believers through scripture, prayer, and sacraments.

4 The final stanza celebrates the future coming of Jesus in glory. The titles King of kings and Prince of Peace come from Revelation 17:14, 19:16 and Isaiah 9:6.

Come, Jesus, Come Morning Star

7.7.7.7.

1 Come, Jesus, come, Morning Star:
   come with rays of joy and peace.
   Word of hope, whom fears would bar,
   from our darkness bring release.

2 Come, Jesus, come, Holy Child:
   come enfleshed in humble birth.
   Word of love, though scorned, reviled,
   give our human life new worth.

3 Come, Jesus, come, living Lord:
   come in prayer and sacraments.
   Word of blessing still outpoured,
   work in ways transcending sense.

4 Come, Jesus, come, King of kings:
   come to rule on earth again.
   Word for whom creation sings,
   "O come, Prince of Peace, and reign."

—Carl P. Daw, Jr.

This hymn is a paraphrase of the Magnificat or Song of Mary from Luke 1:46-55. This canticle is appointed for occasional use at Morning Prayer (BCP, pp. 50, 91-92) and for regular use at Evening Prayer (BCP, pp. 65, 119).

TUNE: This text was written specifically for use with the tune VALET WILL ICH DIR GEBEN (ST. THEODOLPH), which should be sung with somewhat more vigor than it often is with its Palm Sunday text.

REFRAIN: The refrain should always be sung by the full congregation, but the stanzas might well be sung by a cantor or by various groups (e.g. women, men, people seated in certain sections).

1 Mary's song echoes the Song of Hannah (1 Samuel 2:1-10) and anticipates Paul's affirmation that God's strength "is made perfect in weakness" (2 Corinthians 12:9). The latter half of this stanza recalls that Gabriel's greeting to Mary (Luke 1:28) forms the basis of the prayer (the Ave Maria or Hail Mary) with which generations of Christians have called Mary blessed.

2 This stanza could well be illustrated by the great rout of the Egyptians at the Red Sea (Exodus 14:21-31).

3 In addition to Hannah's Song (noted above), this stanza is reminiscent of Psalm 23.

4 For God's covenant with Abraham, see Genesis 17:7, 22:17.

My Soul Proclaims with Wonder

76.76 D

REFRAIN: *My soul proclaims with wonder*
the greatness of the Lord;
rejoicing in God's goodness
my spirit is restored.

1 To me has God shown favor,
    to one the world thought frail,
and every age will echo
    the angel's first "All hail."
        REFRAIN

2 God's mercy shields the faithful
    and saves them from defeat
with strength that turns to scatter
    the proud in their conceit.
        REFRAIN

3 The mighty have been vanquished,
    the lowly lifted up.
The hungry find abundance;
    the rich, an empty cup.
        REFRAIN

4 To Abraham's descendants
    the Lord will steadfast prove,
for God has made with Israel
    a covenant of love.
        REFRAIN

—Carl P. Daw, Jr.

This adaptation of a carol from a fifteenth-century manuscript (Glasgow, Hunterian MS 83) was prepared for *The Hymnal 1982*.

TUNE: The carol has its own tune, NOVA, NOVA, found in the same manuscript as the text.

BURDEN: This refrain is sung at the beginning of the carol and after each stanza. The literal meaning of the Latin is "News! news! 'Hail' is made from 'Eve.'" The wordplay in the Latin hinges on the fact that "Ave" is "Eva" spelled backwards, the theological point being that the angel's greeting to Mary marks the reverse of humanity's sin begun with Eve. If it is preferred to have an English burden, a suitable alternative would be "Tidings! tidings! Promise of salvation!" In congregational use, it is perhaps best to have the congregation sing only the burden and to have a cantor or choir sing the stanzas.

1 This carol is very faithful to the account of the Annunciation in Luke 1:26-38. The original text and tune are given in *Medieval Carols,* ed. John Stevens [Musica Britannica, vol. 4] (London: Stainer and Bell, 1970). p. 111.

2 In the original, the pronoun in this stanza is "I" rather than "he." This may be an indication that the carol was acted out by a group of singers with assigned roles.

5 The original text has reduced the time to six weeks!

6 In the original, Mary's reply is in Latin: "Ecce, ancilla Domini."

Nova, Nova
Ave Fit ex Eva

Irregular with Refrain

BURDEN: *Nova, nova. Ave fit ex Eva.*

1 Gabriel of high degree,
   he was sent from the Trinity,
   to Nazareth in Galilee.
   Nova, nova. BURDEN

2 He met a maiden in that place:
   there he knelt down before her face
   and said, "Hail Mary, full of grace."
   Nova, nova. BURDEN

3 When the maiden heard his song,
   she was filled with confusion strong
   and feared that she had done a wrong.
   Nova, nova. BURDEN

4 Said the angel, "Have no fear,
   by conception without compare
   the Savior Jesus shall you bear."
   Nova, nova. BURDEN

5 "There are yet but six months gone
   since Elizabeth conceived John,
   to be the herald of God's son."
   Nova, nova. BURDEN

6 Said the maiden, "Verily,
   I am your servant right truly,
   the handmaid of the Lord now see."
   Nova, nova. BURDEN

—Hunterian MS. 83, 15th cent.;
adapt. Carl P. Daw, Jr.

CHRISTMAS

TUNE: This text was written specifically for the tune KING'S WESTON.

1 The opening line of this hymn is intended to recall Galatians 4:4 as well as Romans 8:22. The reference to Jesse's root echoes Isaiah 11:1, and the identification of Jesus as the True Vine comes from his self-revelation in John 15:1. The lily and the rose are traditional emblems of the Virgin Mary, and the last two lines allude to the German Christmas hymn *Es ist ein Ros' entsprungen* ("Lo, how a Rose e'er blooming").

2 The mystery of the Incarnation cannot be comprehended by reason; it can only be apprehended by faith.

3 Jesus describes himself as the True Bread/Bread of Heaven in John 6:35-58; "House of Bread" is the literal meaning of the Hebrew word "Bethlehem." In the context of this image, it becomes poignant to recall that a manger is, after all, a feeding trough (Luke 2:7). Jesus both offers eternal life (John 10:28) and calls himself Life (John 11:25, 14:6). The final line of the stanza derives from 1 Corinthians 15:55.

4 The swaddling of an infant was a sign of parental care (Luke 2:7; cf. Ezekiel 16:4, Wisdom of Solomon 7:4). Lines 3-4 are a rearrangement of phrases in the General Thanksgiving of Morning and Evening Prayer (BCP, pp. 58, 71, 101, 125). "Promise of salvation" recalls the meaning of the name Jesus (Matthew 2:21; Luke 2:21,30), and "pledge of peace on earth" echoes the angelic song to the shepherds (Luke 2:14).

WHEN GOD'S TIME HAD RIPENED

65.65.D

1 When God's time had ripened,
   Mary's womb bore fruit,
scion of the Godhead
   sprung from Jesse's root:
so the True Vine branches
   from the lily's stem,
the Rose without blemish
   blooms in Bethlehem.

2 More than mind can fathom,
   limit, or untwine,
this mysterious yoking,
   human and divine;
but what reason fetters,
   faith at length unlocks,
and wise hearts discover
   truth in paradox.

3 As the Bread of Heaven,
   that we might be fed,
chose a manger cradle
   in the House of Bread,
so has Life Eternal
   mingled in the womb
with our mortal nature
   to confound the tomb.

4 For this swaddled infant
   in a humble place
holds our hope of glory
   and our means of grace;
in the Love enfleshed here
   dawns the world's rebirth,
promise of salvation,
   pledge of peace on earth.

—Carl P. Daw, Jr.

This translation of Luther's "Von Himmel hoch" was prepared for the report of the Text Committee for *The Hymnal 1982*. On the floor of the General Convention, however, the translation in the *Lutheran Book of Worship* was substituted as a gesture of ecumenical goodwill.

TUNE: The traditional chorale melody VON HIMMEL HOCH is the obvious choice here.

1 The first three stanzas of this much-reduced version of Luther's hymn are sung by an angel. The rhyme scheme and vocabulary imitate the simple style of Luther's annual Christmas entertainment for his family. The scriptural basis for the angel's song is Luke 2:9-11.

4 The fourth stanza represents the human response to the angel's song. It is roughly analogous to the reaction of the shepherds in Luke 2:15.

FROM HEAVEN HIGH
I COME TO YOU

LM

1 From heaven high I come to you;
   I bring you tidings glad and new,
   such joyous tidings do I bring,
   whereof I will both say and sing.

2 To you this day is born a child:
   born of a maiden mother mild,
   a child so gentle and so rare,
   who brings you joy without compare.

3 Now Christ, the Lord, our God, is born!
   As solace to a world forlorn,
   he comes as Savior, peace to win,
   and he will cleanse you from all sin.

4 All praise to God in heaven above,
   who gives his Son to us in love:
   let us with angel choirs rejoice
   and greet his birth with happy voice.

—Martin Luther
trans. Carl P. Daw, Jr.

This text is a paraphrase of the *Gloria in excelsis,* which may be used as a Canticle at Morning Prayer (BCP, pp. 52, 94-95) or as a Song of Praise in the Eucharist (BCP, pp. 324-325, 356).

TUNE: This texts works well with either DIX or ENGLAND'S LANE.

1   The opening lines of this fourth-century Christian hymn are taken from the song of the angels to the shepherds (Luke 2:14), hence its appropriateness for the Christmas season. The usual English translation, "Glory to God in the highest," can be misunderstood as meaning "highest glory," but the Greek text really alludes to God as dwelling in the highest heavens—i.e. beyond the limits of human comprehension. The opening line of this paraphrase is also a reminder that our understanding of God should not be limited to any pattern of images, even though the traditional Father/Son language has been retained here.

Glory to Our Boundless God

7777.77.

1   Glory to our boundless God,
    who has promised peace on earth.
    God the Father, glorious, strong,
        heaven's Sovereign, Lord of all:
    worship, thanks, and praise we give
        when your glory we recall.

2   Let unceasing praise and prayer
    come to you, Lord Jesus Christ,
    Son of God, incarnate Love,
        Lamb who takes our sin away.
    Risen and exalted Lord,
        hear with mercy as we pray.

3   For in you alone we find
    God's true holiness revealed:
    You alone we claim as Lord,
        Jesus Christ, through whom we see
    God's own fullness manifest
        in the Holy Trinity.

—Carl P. Daw, Jr.

This translation of two stanzas of a longer German hymn by Elizabeth Cruciger (c.1500-1535) was undertaken at the request of Louis Weil.

TUNE: This translation is intended to be used with the original text's proper tune HERR CHRIST DER EINIG GOTTS SOHN in its traditional and more syncopated form (rather than the smoothed-out version found, for example, in the *Lutheran Book of Worship*).

1 This first stanza attempts to capture the original text's affirmation that Christ, the only Son, "sprung from [God's] own heart" in fulfillment of the scriptures has become the Morning Star that shines more brightly than any other. The imagery echoes a number of Johannine themes (e.g. John 1:14,18: 3:16-17; 1 John 4:9; Revelation 22:16). It can also be regarded as a meditation on the second paragraph of the Nicene Creed (BCP, pp. 326-327, 358-359).

2 The Incarnation is not simply the Nativity but includes the whole sweep of Christ's life, death and resurrection. The language here echoes Hebrews 1:2 and also suggests a sentence from the *Te Deum:* "You overcame the sting of death / and opened the kingdom of heaven to all believers" (BCP, p. 96).

FROM GOD ALONE BEGOTTEN

76.76.77.6

1 From God alone begotten,
     Christ came forth from glory,
   Love's own eternal offspring,
     theme of sacred story:
   this brightest star of morning
   still shines, the heavens adorning
     with the light of God's peace.

2 Joined with our human nature,
     born as time was waning,
   hope for sinners who ponder
     God in glory reigning:
   death's power was shattered for us,
   heaven's gates unlocked before us,
     life restored and made new.

—Elizabeth Cruciger:
trans. Carl P. Daw, Jr.

This hymn grew out of a conversation with the Rev. Constance Hammond, who serves in a refugee ministry, about the need for a hymn incorporating concern for displaced people.

TUNE: This text works well with either PLEADING SAVIOR or IN BABILONE.

1 This stanza recasts the terse narrative of Matthew 1:13-15, the only biblical account of the Flight into Egypt. The prophetic utterance mentioned here is Hosea 11:1. The epithets for Joseph and Mary are intentionally reversed from the usual gender stereotypes.

2 The second stanza attempts to balance the narrative of the first stanza by dealing with the journey of the Holy Family from an interior perspective, and thus to connect it with a broad range of experience.

3 The best-known teaching of Jesus emphasizing hospitality for strangers is undoubtedly the description of the Great Judgment in Matthew 25:31-46. But this is far from the only biblical injunction on this subject (see Isaiah 58:7; Hebrews 13:2; 1 Peter 4:9; 3 John 5-8).

Gentle Joseph Heard a Warning

87.87.D

1 Gentle Joseph heard a warning
   from an angel in the night;
valiant Mary, maiden mother,
   roused from sleep, prepared for flight:
thus the Christ-child's family lived out
   what the prophet had foretold,
that he might be called from Egypt
   as God's people were of old.

2 Targets of a tyrant's army,
   seeking safety, fleeing strife,
leaving house and land and kindred,
   spurred by dreams of peaceful life;
through the desert of unknowing
   and the night of doubt they went,
guided by God's promised presence,
   by that trust made confident.

3 Give us, God, such faith and courage
   when we move from place to place,
and to those who come among us,
   make us channels of your grace.
Let us see in every stranger
   refugees from Bethlehem,
help us offer each one welcome
   and receive the Christ in them.

—Carl P. Daw, Jr.

EPIPHANY

"Epiphany" means "manifestation" or "showing forth," and this hymn for the Epiphany season explores a series of important occasions when Jesus was revealed to the world as God's Anointed One. This hymn could be used one stanza at a time as a sequence hymn on the Sundays when the Gospel corresponds to the events which the respective stanzas celebrate. Alternatively, it works especially well in its entirety on the first and last Sundays of the season.

TUNE: This text can be sung effectively to SALZBURG or to ABERYSTWYTH.

1   In Western Christianity, the Feast of the Epiphany (January 6) centers on the coming of the Magi or Wise Men (Matthew 2:1-12), which is treated as the essential manifestation of the Messiah/Christ to the Gentiles. The symbolic interpretations of the three gifts has become traditional.

2   In Eastern Christianity, the primary occasion of manifestation of Christ is at his baptism by John (see the notes for "Mark how the Lamb of God's self-offering," p.45). Recent liturgical revisions in Western churches now provide for the prominent celebration of this event, which was formerly neglected. (Consider, for example, how few hymns deal with this topic.)

3   The third important occasion of manifestation was what John's gospel treats as the first "sign" or miracle: the changing of water to wine at the wedding feast at Cana (John 2:1-11). The latter part of this stanza alludes to the lections about Jesus' healing and teaching which form the Gospels for most of the remaining Sundays of the season.

4   The last Sunday of this season recalls the Transfiguration, an occasion of revelation to the disciples of the glory that lay beyond the agony of the cross. See further the notes to "We have come at Christ's own bidding," p.49.

SING OF GOD MADE MANIFEST

77.77.D

1 Sing of God made manifest
in a child robust and blest,
to whose home in Bethlehem
where a star had guided them,
magi came and gifts unbound,
signs mysterious and profound:
myrrh and frankincense and gold
grave and God and king foretold.

2 Sing of God made manifest
when at Jordan John confessed,
"I should be baptized by you,
but your bidding I will do."
Then from heaven a double sign—
dove-like Spirit, voice divine—
hailed the true Anointed One:
"This is my beloved Son."

3 Sing of God made manifest
when Christ came as wedding-guest
and at Cana gave a sign,
turning water into wine;
further still was love revealed
as he taught, forgave, and healed,
bringing light and life to all
who would listen to God's call.

4 Sing of God made manifest
on the cloud-capped mountain's crest,
where the Law and Prophets waned
so that Christ alone remained:
glimpse of glory, pledge of grace,
given as Jesus set his face
towards the waiting cross and grave,
sign of hope that God would save.

—Carl P. Daw, Jr.

This is a hymn for the First Sunday after the Epiphany, which always celebrates the Baptism of Jesus. In the tradition of the Eastern Orthodox churches, this (rather than the coming of the magi) is the primary event of God's self-revelation in Jesus Christ.

TUNE: This text was written to be sung to RENDEZ À DIEU.

1 The Baptism of Jesus is narrated in Matthew 3:13-17/Mark 1:9-11/Luke 3:21-22.

2 All three synoptic gospels immediately follow the accounts of Jesus' baptism by John with the temptation in the wilderness (Matthew 4:1-2/Mark 1:12-13/Luke 4:1-2). The separation of these episodes in the liturgical calendar (the temptation accounts are not read until the First Sunday of Lent) has obscured a fundamental pattern of the Christian life: i.e. that times of blessing are often followed abruptly by times of adversity. Our experience of such ups and downs is not a sign of spiritual failure but a part of the rhythm of our pilgrimage of faith.

3 The Baptism of Christ is one of the regular occasions for baptisms and for the making and renewing of baptismal vows. As Jesus' baptism was the beginning of his earthly ministry, so our baptisms mark the beginning of our calling to serve Christ. By our baptism we are incorporated into the eternal priesthood of Christ which is entrusted to his Body, the Church. The latter half of this stanza recalls the traditional renunciations and affirmations of the baptismal promises (BCP, pp. 302-303).

MARK HOW THE LAMB
OF GOD'S SELF-OFFERING

98.98.D

1 Mark how the Lamb of God's self-offering
  our human sinfulness takes on
in the birth-waters of the Jordan
  as Jesus is baptized by John.
Hear how the voice from heaven thunders,
  "Lo, this is my beloved Son."
See how in dove-like form the Spirit
  descends on God's Anointed One.

2 From this assurance of God's favor
  Jesus goes to the wilderness,
there to endure a time of testing
  that readied him to teach and bless.
So we, by water and the Spirit
  baptized into Christ's ministry,
are often led to paths of service
  through mazes of adversity.

3 Grant us, O God, the strength and courage
  to live the faith our lips declare;
bless us in our baptismal calling;
  Christ's royal priesthood help us share.
Turn us from every false allegiance,
  that we may trust in Christ alone:
raise up in us a chosen people
  transformed by love to be your own.

—Carl P. Daw, Jr.

This hymn is a paraphrase of Canticle 11: The Third Song of Isaiah, which is appointed for use at Morning Prayer (BCP, pp. 87-88).

TUNE: This text was written to be sung to THE THIRD TUNE by Tallis.

1 The first stanza is based on Isaiah 60:1-3. Both the specific reference to kings in the final line and the general emphasis on light and revelation make this hymn especially suitable for use during the season of Epiphany.

2 The images of this stanza are drawn from Isaiah 60:11a,14c,18.

3 This stanza paraphrases Isaiah 60:19.

Rise Up and Shine!
Your Light Has Come

CMD

1 Rise up and shine! Your light has come;
   God's glory breaks like dawn.
For though the earth be cloaked in night
   and gloom shrouds everyone,
yet over you the Lord will rise,
   with glory gleaming clear,
till nations turn to seek your light
   and humbled kings draw near.

2 Fling wide your gates, both day and night;
   no more keep watch or guard.
You will be called God's holy hill,
   the City of the Lord.
No sound of strife will plague your land,
   nor harm besiege your ways;
"Salvation" will you name your walls,
   and all your portals "Praise."

3 No more will you implore the sun
   to shed by day its light,
nor will you need the changeful moon
   to glisten through the night.
Your glory then will be your God,
   whose light will never cease.
Rise up and shine! Your light has come
   to give you joy and peace.

—Carl P. Daw, Jr.

This text was commissioned by the Church of the Transfiguration in Dallas.

TUNE: Because it was anticipated that a tune would be commissioned for this text, no particular tune was originally associated with it. Several well-known tunes (e.g. ABBOT'S LEIGH, HYFRYDOL, IN BABILONE) can be used effectively.

1 Throughout this hymn there is an implicit comparison between the attitudes and assumptions of the disciples on the Mount of the Transfiguration and the expectations of presentday Christians as they gather for worship.

2 The second stanza treats the Transfiguration narrative (Matthew 17:1-9; Mark 9:2-9: Luke 9:28-36) as remembered and made present (*anamnesis*). The water-imagery ("bathed in light," "drenched in brightness") is intended to suggest the parallels between the Transfiguration and the Baptism of Christ. These two events stand respectively as the last and the first of the Sundays after the Epiphany, and they are significantly united by being the only two occasions when a heavenly voice declared divine approval of Jesus. (I am grateful to the Rev. Dr. Thomas Talley for calling the latter point to my attention.)

3 Peter is the spiritual ancestor of everyone who has been granted some special religious experience and then hopes to recreate it by going back to the same place or reading another book by the same author or singing the same hymn again. All three synoptic accounts underscore the importance of returning to ministry in the world by following the account of the Transfiguration with the healing of the epileptic boy (Matthew 17:14-18; Mark 9:14-27; Luke 9:37-43).

WE HAVE COME AT CHRIST'S OWN BIDDING

87.87.D

1 We have come at Christ's own bidding
      to this high and holy place,
   where we wait with hope and longing
      for some token of God's grace.
   Here we pray for new assurance
      that our faith is not in vain,
   searching like those first disciples
      for a sign both clear and plain.

2 Light breaks in upon our darkness,
      splendor bathes the flesh-joined Word,
   Moses and Elijah marvel
      as the heavenly voice is heard.
   Eyes and hearts behold with wonder
      how the Law and Prophets meet:
   Christ, with garments drenched in brightness,
      stands transfigured and complete.

3 Strengthened by this glimpse of glory,
      fearful lest our faith decline,
   we like Peter find it tempting
      to remain and build a shrine.
   But true worship gives us courage
      to proclaim what we profess,
   that our daily lives may prove us
      people of the God we bless.

—Carl P. Daw, Jr.

LENT

This text was commissioned for the 1987 Diocesan Choir Camp of the Diocese of Connecticut by its director, James Barry. It was premiered there in an anthem setting by David Ashley White.

TUNE: Of the many Short Metre tunes available, FRANCONIA, ST. BRIDE, and SOUTHWELL seem to work best with this text.

1 This text attempts to reclaim the original understanding of Lent as a time for preparing catechumens for Baptism and penitents for reconciliation at the Easter Vigil (cf. BCP, pp. 264-265). The prayer for renewed hearts is intended to echo Jeremiah 31:31-34.

2 The gift of the Holy Spirit in Baptism is recalled here, with allusions to the Lukan emphasis on the Spirit's power (*dynamos*), e.g. Acts 1:8. The last two lines relate what Gerard Manley Hopkins called the "inscape" of human life to the surrounding natural landscape.

3 "Fullness of joy" is a phrase from Psalm 16:11, but it is used here to suggest the idea of Romans 15:29. The latter part of this stanza is drawn from Romans 6:3-4.

4 "Three-personed God" recalls the opening line of John Donne's Holy Sonnet XIV: "Batter my heart, three-personed God..." and "all our searching ends" reflects T.S Eliot's lines in *The Four Quartets:*

> We shall not cease from exploration
> And the end of all our exploring
> Will be to arrive where we started
> And know the place for the first time.

(Little Gidding, 11. 241-244)

Restore in Us, O God

S.M.

1 Restore in us, O God,
    the splendor of your love;
  renew your image in our hearts,
    and all our sins remove.

2 O Spirit, wake in us
    the wonder of your power;
  from fruitless fear unfurl our lives
    like springtime bud and flower.

3 Bring us, O Christ, to share
    the fullness of your joy;
  baptize us in the risen life
    that death cannot destroy.

4 Three-personed God, fulfill
    the promise of your grace,
  that we, when all our searching ends,
    may see you face to face.

—Carl P. Daw, Jr.

This hymn is a paraphrase of Canticle 14: A Song of Penitence (BCP, pp. 90-91), which is appointed for use at Morning Prayer and is noted as "especially suitable in Lent." It is drawn from the apocryphal psalm, The Prayer of Manasseh 1-2,4,6-7,11-15.

TUNE: This text was written to be sung to ST. GEORGE'S (WINDSOR).

1 In order to keep the language of this paraphrase inclusive, the phrase "God of Abraham, Isaac, and Jacob" has become "God of covenant and grace."

2 If the attribution of this prayer to Manasseh is accepted, the sins being confessed here are described in 2 Kings 21:1-18 and 1 Chronicles 33:1-20.

3 God's power is not shown in banishing the sinner to Sheol or Hades (cf. Psalm 63:9) but in granting mercy.

Sovereign Maker of All Things

77.77.D

1 Sovereign Maker of all things,
    God of covenant and grace,
every creature knows your power,
    quakes with fear before your face.
But your mercy far exceeds
    what our minds can comprehend;
deep compassion stays your hand,
    chastening not, though we offend.

2 You have promised to forgive
    contrite sinners who repent;
so I come with humbled heart,
    by your word made confident.
I have sinned, Lord, I have sinned:
    well I know my wickedness.
Yet I make this prayer to you:
    Lord, forgive me, heal, and bless.

3 Let me not be lost in sin,
    banished to eternal night;
God who hears the penitent,
    let your goodness show your might.
Though I be unworthy, Lord,
    your great mercy will I claim,
till I join the hosts above
    who forever praise your name.

—Carl P. Daw, Jr.

This hymn is a paraphrase of Canticle 10: The Second Song of Isaiah with is appointed for use at Morning Prayer (BCP, pp. 86-87).

TUNE: This text is intended for use with ARISE (*Songs for Celebration*) or RESTORATION.

REFRAIN: The refrain is based on Isaiah 55:6-7. It is intended to be sung before the first stanza and after each stanza.

1 This stanza paraphrases Isaiah 55:8-9. To emphasize the divine voice of the stanzas (as distinguished from the prophetic voice of the refrain), it might be effective to have the stanzas sung by a cantor or choir and the refrain sung by the congregation.

2 This stanza is drawn from Isaiah 55:10-11.

SEEK THE LORD, WHOSE WILLING PRESENCE

87.87

REFRAIN: *Seek the Lord, whose willing presence*
moves your heart to make appeal.
Turn from wickedness and evil;
God will pardon, cleanse, and heal.

1 "For my thoughts are not like your thoughts,"
     says the Lord, "nor your ways mine.
 Farther still than earth from heaven
     are things human from divine."
         REFRAIN

2 "As the life-charged dew of heaven
     births the seed and stirs the mill,
 so my word goes forth with power
     to perfect my gracious will."
         REFRAIN

—Carl P. Daw, Jr.

TUNE:This text works well with THE THIRD TUNE or ST. MATTHEW.

1 This hymn was written as a means of pulling together some of the themes from the Lenten readings from the Hebrew Scriptures. The first stanza therefore begins with creation and moves to the image of new creation which shapes the first reading on Lent V in all three years (Ezekiel 37:1-14; Jeremiah 34:31-34; Isaiah 43:16-21).

2 The second stanza alludes to the calling and testing of Abraham (Genesis 12:1-8; 22:1-14) as well as to the Israelites' wandering in the wilderness and the water from the rock (Exodus 17:1-7). It also incorporates an echo of Psalm 130.

3 The third stanza brings together the covenants with Noah (Genesis 9:8-17), with Abraham (Genesis 15:1-12, 17 18), and with Moses (Exodus 3:1-5) and the giving of the Law (Exodus 20:1-17). It concludes with another echo of Jeremiah 34:31-34.

O GOD WHO GIVES US LIFE AND BREATH

C.M.D.

1 O God who gives us life and breath,
    who shapes us in the womb,
 who guards our lives from birth to death,
    then leads us from the tomb:
 deliver us from fears that kill
    the life we have from you;
 help us to know your Spirit still
    is making all things new.

2 O God who calls your people out,
    to venture and to dare,
 to plumb the bleak abyss of doubt
    and find you even there:
 when we despair in wandering
    through wastes of empty lies,
 refresh us with the living spring
    of hope that never dies.

3 O God of covenant and law,
    revealed in cloud and flame,
 your mighty deeds evoke our awe;
    we dare not speak your Name.
 Yet we by faith are drawn to you
    and will your people prove,
 as on our hearts you write anew
    the covenant of love.

—Carl P. Daw, Jr.

The first stanza of this paraphrase of Psalm 42:1-7 was written to provide a new text for an anthem setting David Ashley White had originally composed for another set of words. The other two stanzas were written in the same metre for the present collection.

TUNE: This text can be used effectively with tunes as varied as Gibbons' SONG 4, Carl Schalk's FLENTGE, and Monk's EVENTIDE.

1 This psalm has long been associated with Baptism in Christian tradition, and images of deer at fountains are among the oldest surviving decorations of baptisteries. This text is therefore especially appropriate to use in emphasizing Lent as a season of preparation for Baptism at the Easter Vigil (when it is one of the possible psalms associated with the lessons).

2 As the first stanza is especially appropriate for the baptismal themes of Lent, the second stanza recalls the reconciling of penitents who long to rejoin the worshiping community. (Cf. the Ash Wednesday exhortation, BCP, pp. 264-265.)

3 The final stanza concludes with a resolve of trust in God alone and serves as a reminder that the characteristic shape of Lent is repentance leading to faith.

AS PANTING DEER DESIRE THE WATERBROOKS

10.10.10.10

1 As panting deer desire the waterbrooks
    when wandering in a dry and desert place,
so yearns my thirsty soul for you, O God,
    and longs at last to see you face to face.

2 Both day and night my tears have been my food,
    while scoffers taunt me, "Where is your God now?"
My soul dissolves as I recall the throng
    whose pilgrim hymns I led to Zion's brow.

3 Why are you heavy-hearted, O my soul?
    And why are you so mired in deep discord?
Still put your hope and trust in God alone,
    whom I will praise, my Savior and my Lord.

—Carl P. Daw, Jr.

HOLY WEEK

TUNE: This text was written specifically for the DAKOTA INDIAN CHANT (LACQUIPARLE).

1 The essentially formulaic approach of this text is grounded in the conviction that the events of Holy Week remain sufficiently powerful in themselves and need no elaboration in their telling. The elements of place, posture, kingship, vegetation, clothing, and language generate a narrative matrix which is simultaneously stark and emotive. The details of the triumphal entry of Palm Sunday can be found in Matthew 21:7-9/Mark 11:7-10/Luke 19:35-40/John 12:12-19.

2 The mocking of Christ is told in Matthew 27:27-31/Mark 15:16-20/John 19:1-3.

3 The crucifixion is described in Matthew 27:33-44/Mark 15:22-32/Luke 23:33-43/John 19:17-24. The cry, "My God," appears in Matthew 27:46 and Mark 15:34; "It is finished" occurs only in John 19:30.

Into Jerusalem Jesus Rode

96.99.96

1 Into Jerusalem Jesus rode,
　　triumphant King acclaimed;
　palm branches spread to honor his way,
　garments laid down as tokens of praise;
　shouts of "Hosanna" surged through the throng
　　into Jerusalem.

2 Within Jerusalem Jesus stood
　　masquerade King reviled:
　thorns made a crown (grim satire of truth),
　robe like a wound thrown over his back:
　echoes of "Crucify" filled the air
　　within Jerusalem.

3 Outside Jerusalem Jesus hung,
　　crucified King despised;
　wood formed a cross suspending his life,
　soldiers cast lots to deal out his clothes;
　his lonely cries: "My God"; "It is done"
　　outside Jerusalem.

—Carl P. Daw, Jr.

This hymn was written for St. Mark's Chapel, Storrs, Connecticut, where it has become the parish hymn and is sung every Maundy Thursday.

TUNE: In its home parish, this text is sung to the tune ST. MARK'S CHAPEL, which David Ashley White composed for it. The text also can be used with PANGE LINGUA and PICARDY as well as Gerald Near's LOWRY.

1 The first stanza explores the double sense of "Body of Christ"—consecrated Bread/baptized People—as the starting place for a reflection on the institution of The Lord's Supper. This makes the hymn especially appropriate for Maundy Thursday, but it is no less suitable for any Eucharist. The third line recalls the ancient Jewish dictum that "in the blood is the life" (cf. Genesis 9:4). Line 5 derives from John 1:14. The final line affirms that in this sacrament Christ is truly made present (*anamnesis*).

2 The second stanza centers on the Church's faithful response in worship. The cross of the second line is the one with which each Christian is signed at Baptism (BCP, p. 308). The fifth line affirms the importance of maintaining the apostolic faith.

3 In the third stanza, the Church embraces the eucharistic shape of Christian living. As the forgiven People of God, we are sent forth by the Dismissal: "Go in peace to love and serve the Lord" (BCP, pp. 340, 366). The true measure of worship is that it manifests itself in lives of service.

WITH THE BODY THAT WAS BROKEN

8 7. 8 7. 8 7.

1 With the Body that was broken,
      to the Body who proclaim,
   by the Blood that is life's token,
      for the life found in his Name:
   so the Word-made-flesh has spoken,
      and his presence here we claim.

2 In the cross of Christ confiding,
      by the cross we bear as sign,
   through the Spirit's gifts and guiding,
      with these gifts of bread and wine:
   so the Church in faith abiding
      keeps the feast Christ made divine.

3 Fed by breaking and outpouring,
      joined in breaking-forth of praise,
   given the peace of God's restoring,
      sent in peace to live always:
   so we show forth our adoring
      as God's servants all our days.

—Carl P. Daw, Jr.

This text is a translation and paraphrase of the Latin hymn sung on Maundy Thursday either at the offertory or during the washing of the feet, a ceremony based on the appointed Gospel for the day (John 13:1-15).

TUNE: This text is intended to be sung to its proper plainsong setting UBI CARITAS.

REFRAIN: According to the conventions of good Latin usage, the first clause of the original refrain has no verb (a form of "to be" therefore being implied): "Ubi caritas et amor, Deus ibi est." The version offered here attempts to convey the thrust of the original in idiomatic and inclusive English.

1 The language of the first stanza is reminiscent of 1 John 4:7-12.

2 An emphasis on Christians as members of one Body is a recurrent Pauline theme; see, for example, Romans 12:4-5; 1 Corinthians 12:12-27; Ephesians 4:25.

3 The final stanza echoes the concluding petition of the *Te Deum:* cf. BCP, pp. 53, 96, and "We praise you, O God, and acclaim you as Lord" (p. 119).

WHERE CHARITY AND LOVE INCREASE

12.12.12.12 with Refrain

REFRAIN: *Where charity and love increase,*
                    God is there indeed.

1   Because Christ's love has gathered us and made us one,
      let us now rejoice and be glad in him always.
      And as we fear and love our Lord, the living God,
      so let us love one another with sincere hearts.
                    REFRAIN

2   Joined as members of one Body, let us gather
      without discord or enmity to divide us.
      Let all our petty jealousies and hatred cease,
      that in our midst we may know Christ, our Lord and God.
                    REFRAIN

3   Grant us at last with all your saints to see your face
      in the glory of your presence, O Christ our God,
      the boundless source of all goodness and of all joy,
      through endless ages of ages, for evermore.
                    REFRAIN

—Latin office hymn;
trans. Carl P. Daw, Jr.

TUNE: There is a special sense of starkness conveyed by singing this text to THE CHURCH'S DESOLATION; alternatively, THE THIRD TUNE offers a suitably complex setting of a different kind.

1 The Crucifixion is the undoing of creation: it is marked by darkness, earthquake, and the rending of the Temple veil (Matthew 27:45-56/Mark 15:33-41/Luke 23:44-49).

2 The second stanza meditates on the painful reality of this scene. Line 4, quoted from Shakespeare (*Othello* III.iii.92), takes on special poignancy here. Line 5 is borrowed from "What boundless love, O Carpenter of Nazareth" (p. 155), with allusion to John Donne's "Good Friday, 1613. Riding Westward" (lines 21-22): "Could I behold those hands which span the poles, / And tune all spheres at once, pierced with those holes?" The last two lines of this stanza attempt to mirror John 1:1-5.

3 The third stanza contemplates the immense power of suffering love and the sublime irony of calling this day "Good" Friday.

How Shallow Former Shadows Seem

C.M.D.

1 How shallow former shadows seem
    beside this great reverse
as darkness swallows up the Light
    of all the universe:
creation shivers at the shock,
    the Temple rends its veil,
a pallid stillness stifles time,
    and nature's motions fail.

2 This is no midday fantasy,
    no flight of fevered brain.
With vengeance awful, grim, and real,
    chaos is come again:
the hands that formed us from the soil
    are nailed upon the cross;
the Word that gave us life and breath
    expires in utter loss.

3 Yet deep within this darkness lives
    a Love so fierce and free
that arcs all voids and—risk supreme!—
    embraces agony.
Its perfect testament is etched
    in iron, blood, and wood;
with awe we glimpse its true import
    and dare to call it good.

—Carl P. Daw, Jr.

EASTER

This text was written at the request of Alec Wyton, who later prepared an anthem arrangement of it to SINE NOMINE with brass and tympani (Paraclete Press PPM08702).

TUNE: Either SINE NOMINE or ENGELBERG works well; with the latter tune, only one "alleluia" is required at the end of each stanza.

1. This hymn is a paraphrase of the Easter Canticle which replaces the Invitatory Psalm at Morning Prayer during the Easter season (BCP, pp. 46, 83). The first stanza is drawn from 1 Corinthians 5:7-8.

2. The second stanza is based on Romans 6:9-11.

3. The third stanza paraphrases 1 Corinthians 15:20-22.

God's Paschal Lamb is Sacrificed for Us

10.10.10.10

1 God's Paschal Lamb is sacrificed for us;
 therefore with joy we keep the Easter feast;
 forsaking sin, we share the bread of truth.
  Alleluia, alleluia!

2 Now is Christ raised and will not die again;
 death has no more dominion over him.
 Through him we die to sin and live to God.
  Alleluia, alleluia!

3 In Christ we see the first fruits of the dead:
 though Adam's sin has doomed all flesh to die,
 in Christ's new life shall all be made alive.
  Alleluia, alleluia!

—Carl P. Daw, Jr.

°Paraclete Press PPM 08702A (anthem setting by Alec Wyton)

This is a paraphrase of Canticle 8: The Song of Moses (BCP, p.85), which is translation of Exodus 15:1-6, 11-13, 17-18.

TUNE: This text was written for use with the tune LOBE DEN HERREN.

1   Because this canticle is especially associated with the Easter season, the fourth line interpolates an allusion to 2 Corinthians 5:17 underscoring that connection. The refrain in each stanza is based on Exodus 15:18.

2   God's identity as Creator is reinforced by the deployment of natural forces to defeat the enemy. The paraphrasing in this stanza is intending to recall the Magnificat (especially Luke 1:51-52).

3   Cf. Deuteronomy 26:5-9.

4   "Constant love" attempts to translate the Hebrew word *hesed* (RSV "steadfast love"), the unwavering care and regard God shows for the covenant people. The "holy place" is Mount Zion, which became the site of the Temple.

SING TO THE LORD, WHO HAS VANQUISHED THE HORSE AND THE WARRIOR

14.14.478

1 Sing to the Lord, who has vanquished the
        horse and the warrior;
    hurled in the sea now lies Israel's scourge and
        annoyer!
    Be glad and sing,
    for God has done a new thing;
        so shall the Lord reign for ever.

2 Blessed be your Name, O God, ever our
        strength and defender!
    Snared in the flood, the proud forces of
        Pharaoh surrender;
    like stones they fall,
    and the deep swallows them all:
        so shall the Lord reign for ever.

3 Who can compare with your holiness, honor
        and glory?
    Your wondrous deeds are the splendor of your
        people's story;
    your mighty arm
    saves your beloved from harm:
        so shall the Lord reign for ever.

4 With constant love, O God, you set us free and
        you fed us,
    bringing us safely to dwell in the land where
        you led us,
    guarded by grace,
    planted in your holy place:
        so shall the Lord reign for ever.

—Carl P. Daw, Jr.

TUNE: This text works well with MORNING SONG.

1 The first stanza is based on John 20:19-31, which is always the Gospel on the Second Sunday of Easter. The possibility of a connection between Thomas' doubt and his experience of mistaken identity as a twin (John 11:16) came to my attention in a sermon by the Rev. John H. Hatcher, Jr.

2 Cf. "Praise God whose providential awkwardness," p. 97, and the notes to the second stanza of "Let kings and prophets yield their name," p. 139.

3 The final word of this stanza is an intentional pun: the Good News of God in Christ is not bound either by our physical senses or by commonsense expectations.

WHEN THOMAS HEARD THE STRANGE REPORT

86.86.86

1 When Thomas heard the strange report
    that someone had appeared
and stood among Christ's frightened friends,
    he balked and darkly feared
that they mistook (as twins know well)
    and so were falsely cheered.

2 Thanks be to God for honest doubt,
    for faith that dares to ask
the questions born in lively minds
    and will not smugly bask
in superficial piety
    or hide behind a mask.

3 Give us, like Thomas, faith that seeks
    to honor evidence
but still is open to God's truth
    and welcomes the immense
surprise that Christ will not remain
    within the tomb of sense.

—Carl P. Daw, Jr.

This hymn was one of the results of preparing a series of sermons for the Easter season based on parallels between the post-Resurrection appearances of Christ and the actions of the Church as the Body of Christ in the world today. Each stanza could be used separately as a sequence hymn on the respective Sunday for which it provides a commentary on the appointed Gospel.

TUNE: The most appealing tune melodically is KING'S LYNN, but there is much to commend AURELIA because of its strong association with "The Church's one foundation" (that connotation adds interesting dimensions to the singing of this text). The tunes LIGHT and LLANGOFFAN can also be used effectively.

1 This image is based on John 20:19-31, which is unvaryingly the Gospel on the Second Sunday of Easter.

2 The Third Sunday of Easter always includes one of the post-Resurrection meals (Luke 24:13-35: Luke 24:36b-48; John 21:11-14).

3 The third stanza is particularly suited to the Seventh Sunday of Easter (the Sunday after Ascension Day), which takes as its Gospel every year some part of the "high priestly prayer" in John 17. These passages often deal with what it means for Christians to be in the world but not of the world.

O RISEN CHRIST, STILL WOUNDED

76.76.D

1 O risen Christ, still wounded,
    triumphant, broken Life,
whose glory holds within it
    the scars of human strife:
may we your living Body,
    the Church that bears your name,
be likewise true in bearing
    the marks of hurt and shame.

2 O risen Christ, still feeding
    with fish and bread and wine,
whose care becomes incarnate
    when word and deed combine:
so may your Church be mindful
    of every human need,
to nourish souls and bodies
    and hungry hearts to feed.

3 O risen Christ, still reigning,
    to let Love's power be shown,
you took our human nature
    and made a cross your throne:
convert your Church from thinking
    that wordly power is good;
awake us to discover
    true strength in servanthood.

—Carl P. Daw, Jr.

PENTECOST

This text was written at the request of the Text Committee for *The Hymnal 1982*.

TUNE: This text was written expressly for Peter Cutts' tune BRIDEGROOM. Since its appearance in *The Hymnal 1982* it has received anthem settings by David Ashley White (Choristers Guild CGA-352) and Shirley W. McRae (Concordia 98-2757). It has also been translated into Spanish for inclusion in *Albricias*, a collection of hymns published by the National Hispanic Office of the Episcopal Church.

1 In the writing of this text, the content of the refrain became obvious first. Once it was clear that each stanza would lead up to a prayer for the coming of the Holy Spirit, the stanzas fell into several natural clusters of images. The first stanza portrays *how* the Spirit comes. The opening phrase of the hymn was suggesting by recalling a discussion in Louis Evely's book *A Religion for Our Time* (New York: Herder and Herder, 1968) "the image of the dove was chosen not because of the shape of the bird, but because of the moan. The dove murmurs all the time. It is because the Holy Spirit moans all the time that he is represented under the form of a dove; it is a verbal and not a plastic image" (p. 21). Evely goes on to quote Romans 8:26 and could have given further evidence by referring to Isaiah 38:14 or 59:11, which use the image of the moaning dove as metaphors for praying in distress. The images of wind and flame derive from the account of the first Christian Pentecost (Acts 2:2-3). "Vigor" and "might" are intended to recall the Lucan emphasis on the power (*dynamos*) of the Spirit.

2 The second stanza turns to the *where* or *to whom* aspect of the Spirit's coming. The various images of the Church are Pauline (the Body of Christ: Romans 12:4-5, 1 Corinthians 12:12-13 [cf. Ephesians 4:23]), Johannine (Christ as the True Vine: John 15:1-5), and Lucan (the assembled community: Acts 2:1). Although their chronologies differ, both Luke and John indicate that the Holy Spirit is a gift from God and a sign of divine empowerment (Acts 1:8; John 20:22-23).

3 The third stanza is concerned with the purposes for which the Spirit is given (the *why*): for reconciliation, prayer (Romans 8:26), divine power (Acts 1:8), and quiet confidence.

LIKE THE MURMUR OF THE DOVE'S SONG

8 7. 8 7. 6

1 Like the murmur of the dove's song,
   like the challenge of her flight,
   like the vigor of the wind's rush,
   like the new flame's eager might:
      come, Holy Spirit, come.

2 To the members of Christ's Body,
   to the branches of the Vine,
   to the Church in faith assembled,
   to her midst as gift and sign:
      come, Holy Spirit, come.

3 With the healing of division,
   with the ceaseless voice of prayer,
   with the power to love and witness,
   with the peace beyond compare:
      come, Holy Spirit, come.

—Carl P. Daw, Jr.

TUNE: This text was written to be sung to ABERYSTWYTH.

1 The opening petition draws together the two accounts of the giving of the Holy Spirit (John 20:19-23: Acts 2:1 4) by suggesting that the common condition of the disciples beforehand was fear (as is often our condition still). The bestowing of the Spirit is a further expression of the life-giving freedom made known by Christ's resurrection. Line 3 draws on 2 Corinthians 3:17. "Power" in line 4 alludes to *dynamos,* one of the most frequently used attributes of the Spirit in the New Testament. Pentecost represents the reversal of Babel, when human pride attempted to storm heaven and was thwarted by the confusion of tongues (Genesis 11:19), because here everyone was able to understand the preaching of the Christians (Acts 2:5-21). For a discussion of line 6, see the beginning of notes on "Like the murmur of the dove's song" (p. 85). The dove and the flame are two of the principal images of the Holy Spirit; the last two lines here are intended to echo the final couplet of the fifth of John Donne's *Holy Sonnets:* "And burn me, O Lord, with a fiery zeal / Of thee and thy house, which doth in eating heal."

2 The technical term for the interrelatedness of the Persons of the Trinity is *perichoresis,* a Greek term meaning "dance around." One of the principal meanings of the mystery of the Trinity is that this shared life of the Godhead indicates that life in community is essential for those who are created in God's image. Line 5 recalls that in the languages of the Bible (as well as in many modern ones), the words for "breath" and "spirit" are the same. Line 7 derives from Acts 2:4. The final line echoes the Dismissal of the Eucharist, "Go in peace to love and serve the Lord" (BCP, pp. 340, 366).

Soaring Spirit, Set Us Free

7.7.7.7.D

1 Soaring Spirit, set us free
    from the tyranny of fear;
Life of glorious liberty,
    let your promised power appear:
drown the noise of Babel's tongues
    in the murmur of the dove;
burn away our wasting wrongs
    with the healing fire of love.

2 Unseen Member of the dance
    that unites the Trinity,
let the grace your presence grants
    twine us in like mystery.
Breath of God, our lives inspire
    till our hope and faith increase:
speak through us with tongues of fire:
    send us forth to spread God's peace.

—Carl P. Daw, Jr.

THE MYSTERY
OF GOD

TUNE: This text seems to work best with DIX.

1 The opening line deals with two realities: first, fascination with naming God can become a means of avoiding the experience of God; and second, the name(s) of God are often taken in vain by people who have minimal awareness of God. On the other hand, the stanza goes on to explore the dangers of a false certainty in such matters.

2 The opening line alludes to 1 Kings 19:12 and the second to Job 38:4-7. The third line recalls Exodus 3:1-14.

3 The serene, stylized manner of icons offers a helpful model of discipline and freedom in the search for theological language. The frequently-expressed notion that icons are "windows" or "doors" into the transcendent is a refreshing alternative to the descriptive and denotative assumptions that often attend discussions of language about God.

4 It is extremely important to recognize that all our descriptions of God are inadequate because they attempt to extrapolate the infinite from the finite.

Wondrous God, More Named Than Known

77.77.77

1 Wondrous God, more named than known,
    give us, firm and certain grown,
grace to doubt what we surmise,
    lest we miss the glad surprise
when we find your truth exceeds
    all the forecasts of our creeds.

2 Pregnant Silence, lively Calm,
    Singer of creation's psalm,
great "I AM" of burning bush:
    still resist our urge to push
till you fit the names we choose,
    shadows of the light we lose.

3 Save us from proud, empty claims
    in our zeal to give you names.
Let our notions be expressed
    not to limit but suggest
views that icon-like disclose
    splendor more than we suppose.

4 God not female, God not male,
    God for whom all labels fail,
Truth beyond our verbal games,
    Life too vast to bound with names:
from vain wordlust set us free
    to embrace your mystery.

—Carl P. Daw, Jr.

This text was written for the tenth anniversary celebration of the Northeast Connecticut Chapter of the American Guild of Organists in 1987.

TUNE: For the celebration a tune was written by Cameron Johnson, a member of the AGO chapter. The text has been published in an anthem setting by John Bertalot (Agape AG 7287). Perhaps the most effective tune for general use is GENEVA.

1 The first stanza draws on the account of creation in the 38th chapter of Job; the third and fourth lines especially allude to Job 38:7. The final line is intended as a reminder that one aspect of humanity's creation in the image of God is manifest in creative activity. "Maker" is used here with a conscious reference to its archaic use to mean "poet."

2 The second stanza continues the metaphor of harmony from the first stanza with a sometimes punning use of musical terms, culminating in the last line's allusion to the opening petition of the prayer sometimes attributed to St. Francis of Assisi (BCP, p. 833).

3 Cf. Isaiah 35:10.

GOD OF GRACE AND GOD OF LAUGHTER

8.7.8.7.D

1 God of grace and God of laughter,
    singing worlds from nought to be–
sun and stars and all thereafter
    joined in cosmic harmony:
give us songs of joy and wonder,
    music making hearts rejoice;
let our praises swell like thunder,
    echoing our Maker's voice.

2 When our lives are torn by sadness,
    heal our wounds with tuneful balm;
when all seems discordant madness,
    help us find a measured calm.
Steady us with music's anchor
    when the storms of life increase:
in the midst of hurt and rancor,
    make us instruments of peace.

3 Turn our sighing into singing,
    music born of hope restored:
set our souls and voices ringing,
    tune our hearts in true accord:
till we form a mighty chorus
    joining angel-choirs above,
with all those who went before us,
    in eternal hymns of love.

—Carl P. Daw, Jr.

TUNE: A number of tunes seem to work with this text: HALIFAX, KINGSFOLD, LARAMIE, SALVATION.

1 The governing image here is wrestling with God, as Jacob did at the Jabbok (Genesis 32:24-32) and as the Greek of 1 Timothy 6:12 implies ("struggle" would be a better translation than the usual "fight"). For many people, altering language about God deeply affect their ability to be engaged with God.

2 It is both ironic and appropriate that secular concerns for non-discrimination and equal treatment have given rise to much of the awareness of language which has eventually brought the churches to consider how they use language about people and about God.

3 The final lines of this stanza are based on an experience of the Greek novelist Nikos Kazantzakis, as retold by William Toohey: The novelist was on a remote island visiting a saintly monk and asked him, "Do you still wrestle with the devil, Fr. Makarios?" The monk replied, "Not any longer, my child. I have grown old and the devil has grown old with me. He doesn't have the strength. I now wrestle with God." "With God?" exclaimed Kazantzakis. "And you hope to win?" "No," the monk replied. "I hope to lose." (*Life After Birth: Spirituality for College Students* [New York: Seabury, 1980], pp. 29-30).

O GOD,
ON WHOM WE LOST OUR HOLD

C.M.D.

1 O God, on whom we lost our hold
     when all your names were changed,
 we find our prayers and hymns confused,
     more awkward and estranged.
 Yet there is hope in these new words,
     sweet fruit in bitter rind:
 the promise of a keener faith
     than that we leave behind.

2 The language which we knew so well
     flowed smoothly on the tongue,
 though seldom did we pause to weigh
     how things were said or sung.
 But now the world is showing us
     with stunning clarity
 the problems with the words we used
     to tame a mystery.

3 Dear God, inspire our hearts and minds
     to seek your truth anew,
 and help us with each fresh insight
     to find names fit for you.
 Yet never let us idolize
     the images we choose;
 but as we strive, give us the grace
     to wrestle and to lose.

—Carl P. Daw, Jr.

TUNE: The recommended tune for this text is Carl Shalk's FLENTGE.

1   This hymn was written after reading Martin Thornton's book
    Prayer: A New Encounter (London: Hodder and Stoughton,
    1972). The phrase "providential awkwardness" in the opening
    line is one that Thornton uses several times. The third line
    derives from 1 Corinthians 3:19.

2   The limits of our knowledge and our certainty make us aware
    of our need for God.

3   The opening line echoes Psalm 90:1. The last two lines are
    intended to recall Matthew 6:33 and 1 Corinthians 13:13.

PRAISE GOD, WHOSE PROVIDENTIAL AWKWARDNESS

10 10. 10 10.

1 Praise God, whose providential awkwardness
   defies our human powers of scrutiny,
 whose wisdom looks to us like foolishness,
   whose purposes seem cloaked in mystery.

2 Praise God for what we fail to comprehend,
   for silence and for possibility,
 for timeless memory too deep for words,
   for truth that lurks within reality.

3 Praise God, who gives us restless hearts and minds,
   who still is both our source and resting-place,
 and who endows us with the faith to seek,
   the hope to dare, the love to answer grace.

—Carl P. Daw, Jr.

THE CHURCH'S PRAISE

This text was commissioned for the 1989 celebration of the Twenty-fifth Anniversary of the Consecration of Grace Cathedral, San Francisco, on 20 November 1964.

TUNE: The best tune for these words is probably KING'S LYNN, but they also fit nicely with LIGHT and LLANGLOFFAN.

1 While the opening line could well be suitable to many liturgical spaces, it pertains specifically to the great font and the high altar which balance each other at each end of the Nave of Grace Cathedral. The second half of the first stanza is intended to recall Psalm 29:2 (BCP translation) and Mark 11:17/Isaiah 56:7.

2 The emblem of Grace Cathedral is the dove of the Holy Spirit with seven flames for the Spirit's sevenfold gifts.

3 The phrasing here particularly recalls the story as it is told in John 2:13-17 (with parallels at Matthew 21:12-14; Mark 11:15-19; Luke 19:45-48). The petition which begins the second half of this stanza is intended to evoke the large Chi-Rho in the middle of the central Nave aisle of Grace Cathedral.

O GOD OF FONT AND ALTAR

76.76.D

1 O God of font and altar,
        of music, grandeur, light;
    toward whom the soaring arches
        aspire beyond their height:
    as beauty draws us to you
        within this house of prayer,
    let worship form and feed us
        to help us show your care.

2 O life-bestowing Spirit,
        inspire this hallowed space;
    breathe through us with new fervor
        and fill us with your grace.
    Arouse our lagging spirits,
        enflame our hearts with joy:
    here let a love be kindled
        that death cannot destroy.

3 O Christ, who cleansed the Temple,
        baptize us with your zeal,
    and teach us your compassion
        to love, forgive, and heal.
    Be in our midst to claim us
        and mark us as your own,
    then send us forth in witness
        to make your mercy known.

—Carl P. Daw, Jr.

This text, a paraphrase of Psalm 84, was edited and written at the request of the Text Committee for *The Hymnal 1982*. The first two stanzas are a cento from *The Psalms of David in Meeter* (1650): the remaining two stanzas were written to provide a paraphrase of the entire psalm in the same style.

TUNE: This text can be sung to BROTHER JAMES' AIR or MORNING SONG.

How Lovely
is Thy Dwelling Place

8 6. 8 6. 8 6

1 How lovely is thy dwelling- place,
   O Lord of Hosts, to me!
My thirsty soul desires and longs
   within thy courts to be;
my very heart and flesh cry out,
   O living God, for thee.

2 Beside thine altars, gracious Lord,
   the swallows find a nest;
how happy they who dwell with thee
   and praise thee without rest,
and happy they whose hearts are set
   upon the pilgrim's quest.

3 They who go through the desert vale
   will find it filled with springs,
and they shall climb from height to height
   till Zion's temple rings
with praise to thee, in glory throned,
   Lord God, great King of kings.

4 One day within thy courts excels
   a thousand spent away;
how happy they who keep thy laws
   nor from thy precepts stray,
for thou shalt surely bless all those
   who live the words they pray.

—stanzas 1-2, *The Psalms of David in Meeter*
stanzas 3-4, Carl P. Daw, Jr.

This text was commissioned as an offertory response for the Fourth Presbyterian Church in Chicago.

TUNE: In the congregational hymnal at Fourth Presbyterian Church, this text appears with the tune FOURTH CHURCH written for it by the parish's music director, Morgan Simmons. In other congregations it would be appropriate to use any broad tune in this metre.

1 The triune activity of God as Creator (line 1), Savior (line 2), and Sustainer (line 7) makes possible our human response of thanksgiving and aspiration.

FOR THE LIFE
THAT YOU HAVE GIVEN

87.87.D

For the life that you have given,
    for the love in Christ made known,
with these fruits of time and labor,
    with these gifts that are your own:
here we offer, Lord, our praises;
    heart and mind and strength we bring.
Give us grace to love and serve you,
    living what we pray and sing.

—Carl P. Daw, Jr.

This is a paraphrase of the first seven verses of Psalm 95, which form one of the possible invitatories (the Venite) at the beginning of Morning Prayer (BCP, pp. 44-45, 82).

TUNE: This text was written specifically for use with OLD 124TH.

1   People who are uncomfortable with singing "the Lord" may substitute "our God" in the opening lines of the first two stanzas and "our sovereign God" in the first line of the third stanza.

2-3   The second and third stanzas celebrate the sovereignty God enjoys by virtue of being the Creator of all things. It is interesting to note that the Creator described here is more like that of the second creation account (Genesis 2:4b-25) than the first (Genesis 1:1-2:4a).

COME, LET US SING WITH JOY UNTO THE LORD

10.10.10.10.10

1 Come, let us sing with joy unto the Lord;
   let us be glad and heartily rejoice.
  Into God's presence come with hymns of praise;
  with thankful hearts new psalms and anthems raise,
    till all earth's tongues be joined in one great voice.

2 Great is the Lord, and greatly to be praised,
   sovereign above all powers of heaven and earth.
  Caverns and heights lie both within God's hand,
  who made the sea and molded the dry land,
    and from whose life all creatures have their birth.

3 Come, let us kneel before the Lord our God;
   to our Creator let all hearts draw near.
  This is our God, whose folk and sheep are we,
  whose steadfast love endures eternally.
    Oh, that today you would God's calling hear!

—Carl P. Daw, Jr.

This text provides a paraphrase of the l00th Psalm, which is one of the invitatories at the beginning of Morning Prayer (BCP, pp. 45, 82-83).

TUNE: This text was written to be sung to LEONI.

Be Joyful in the Lord

66. 84. D

1 Be joyful in the Lord;
     be joyful, all you lands.
  With gladness come before the Lord;
     draw near with song.
  Know that the Lord is God,
     who made us and still stands
  to guard the folk, who like a flock,
     to God belong.

2 Approach God's house with thanks
     and fill its courts with praise;
  with awe invoke God's holy Name:
     come and adore.
  The Lord our God is good,
     whose mercy lasts always
  and whose great faithfulness endures
     for evermore.

—Carl P. Daw, Jr.

This hymn is a paraphrase of Canticle 1/12: A Song of Creation, taken from the apocryphal book the Song of the Three Young Men 35-65 (BCP, pp. 47-49, 88-90).

TUNE: This text was written to be sung to MIT FREUDEN ZART.

1 The three stanzas of this hymn correspond to the three major divisions of this canticle in the Book of Common Prayer. The first stanza concerns the cosmic order.

2 The second stanza deals with the earth and its creatures.

3 The third section of the Prayer Book canticle is headed "The People of God." In this hymn the opening line of the third stanza is borrowed from the final apostrophe of the second section of the Prayer Book canticle.

LET ALL CREATION BLESS THE LORD

87.87.887

1 Let all creation bless the Lord,
     till heav'n with praise is ringing.
   Sun, moon, and stars, peal out a chord,
     stir up the angels' singing.
   Sing, wind and rain! Sing, snow and sleet!
   Make music, day, night, cold, and heat:
     exalt the God who made you.

2 All living things upon the earth,
     green fertile hills and mountains,
   sing to the God who gave you birth;
     be joyful, springs and fountains.
   lithe water-life, bright air-borne birds,
   wild roving beasts, tame flocks and herds:
     exalt the God who made you.

3 O men and women everywhere
     lift up a hymn of glory:
   all you who know God's steadfast care,
     tell out salvation's story.
   No tongue be silent; sing your part,
   you humble souls and meek of heart:
     exalt the God who made you.

—Carl P. Daw, Jr.

This hymn is a paraphrase of the *Benedictus es, Domine,* Canticle 2/13 (BCP, pp. 49, 90), which is appointed for use at Morning Prayer. It comes from the Apocrypha (Song of the Three Young Men 29-34).

TUNE: By virtue of its doxological associations, OLD 100th is perhaps the best Long Metre tune for this text. It also works well with THE EIGHTH TUNE (TALLIS' CANON).

1   This paraphrase is intentionally written in inclusive language, so that the phrase "God of our fathers" has been recast to reflect its essential point, i.e. God's covenant faithfulness through many generations.

2   The second stanza celebrates the Temple's representation of God's throne flanked by cherubim (Psalm 80:1, 99:1; Isaiah 37:16), which were portrayed with outstretched wings on the Ark of the Covenant (Exodus 25:18-20, 37:6-9: Numbers 7:89: 1 Samuel 4:4; 1 Kings 6:23-28, 8:6-7). It is possible that this canticle was composed as a hymn of praise for the restoration of Temple worship. Cf. Psalm 150:1 and Isaiah 6:1.

3   In the third stanza the focus returns to the transcendent God implied by the splendor of the earthly Temple. The Trinitarian conclusion is, of course, a Christian addition.

GLORY TO YOU, OUR FAITHFUL GOD

L.M.

1 Glory to you, our faithful God,
  for you are worthy of all praise;
  blest be the radiance of your Name:
  we will exalt you evermore.

2 Glory to you in splendor shrined,
  resplendent on your royal throne,
  dwelling between the Cherubim:
  we will exalt you evermore.

3 Glory to you, in heaven's height,
  guarding the deep with watchful care.
  Glory to you, our Triune God;
  we will exalt you evermore.

—Carl P. Daw, Jr.

This is a paraphrase of Canticle 18: A Song to the Lamb (BCP, pp. 93-94), which is appointed for use at Morning Prayer. The canticle is drawn from Revelation 4:11, 5:9-10, 13.

TUNE: This text was written for use with the tune ROUEN.

1 The latter part of the second line is an intentional allusion to Robert Robinson's well-known hymn, "Come, thou fount of every blessing." "Bidding" and "called" are reminders that Genesis 1:1-2:3 describes creation as the response to God's command.

2 The new creation accomplished by Christ's death and resurrection has brought forth a redeemed and priestly community drawn from all the peoples of the earth.

3 It would probably be a mistake to regard the absence of reference to the Holy Spirit in this apocalyptic hymn as a deficiency of Trinitarian doctrine; that is not really the purpose here. Rather, the point is being made that the salvific work of Christ restores creation to its intended fullness.

SPENDOR AND HONOR, MAJESTY AND POWER

11. 11. 11. 5

1 Splendor and honor, majesty and power,
are yours, O Lord God, fount of every blessing,
for by your bidding was the whole creation
  called into being.

2 Praised be the true Lamb, slain for our redemption,
by whose self-offering we are made God's people:
a priestly kingdom, from all tongues and nations,
  called to God's service.

3 To the Almighty, throned in heavenly splendor,
and to the Savior, Christ our Lamb and Shepherd,
be adoration, praise, and glory given,
  now and for ever.

—Carl P. Daw, Jr.

This hymn is a paraphrase of Canticle 19: The Song of the Redeemed (BCP, p. 94), which comes from Revelation 15:3-4 and is appointed for use at Morning Prayer.

TUNE: This text was written for MORNING SONG, though it also works well with Howells' SANCTA CIVITAS.

1 This apocalyptic hymn weaves together phrases from Hebrew scripture and places them in the mouth of the redeemed in the vision of Revelation. In the first stanza, there are allusions to Psalm 92:5, 98:1, Deuteronomy 32:4, and Psalm 145:17.

2 The second stanza includes allusions to Jeremiah 10:7 and Psalm 86:9-10.

WE MARVEL AT YOUR MIGHTY DEEDS

86.86.86

1 We marvel at your mighty deeds,
   Lord God of time and space;
we praise your truth and righteousness,
   great King of boundless grace:
for through each wonder and decree
   your steadfast love we trace.

2 Who shall not pay you homage, Lord,
   and bless your sacred Name?
Because your just and holy works
   your sovereign power proclaim,
all nations will at last draw near
   and you alone acclaim.

—Carl P. Daw, Jr.

This hymn is a paraphrase of the *Te Deum laudamus*, Canticle 7/21 (BCP, pp. 52-53, 95-96), appointed for use at Morning Prayer, especially on Sundays. Because this is one of the most festive canticles, it is among those recommended for use at the Eucharist of the Easter Vigil (BCP, p. 294).

TUNE: This text was written with CAELITES PLAUDANT in mind. It should also work well with CHRISTE SANCTORUM or ROUEN.

1   This ancient hymn of the Church is generally agreed to date from about the fourth century, though there are varying traditions regarding its authorship. The tone of the whole is reminiscent of the heavenly worship described in the Revelation to John.

2   The presence of the Sanctus in the *Te Deum* strengthens the argument that it may originally have been composed as a eucharistic prayer. Compare the language and imagery here with Isaiah 6:3 and Revelation 4:8; 7:9-17.

3   The epithet "worthy" connects this canticle with Revelation 4:11, 5:9-10 (see "Splendor and honor, majesty and power," p. 115). The attributes of the Holy Spirit adopted for this paraphrase are drawn from John 14:16-17, 15:26.

4   The phrase "king of glory," though implied by various passages, does not occur in the New Testament: it probably derives from Christological interpretations of Psalm 24. The image of death's sting comes from 1 Corinthians 15:55-56.

5   The image of Christ as judge comes from Matthew 25:31-46, John 5:22, and related passages. It is perhaps worth noting that saints and angels are distinct orders of being: contrary to some forms of popular piety, human beings do not become angels in the life to come.

WE PRAISE YOU, O GOD, AND ACCLAIM YOU AS LORD

11.11.11.5

1 We praise you, O God, and acclaim you as Lord.
   All creatures bless you, Father everlasting:
   to you all angels, all the host of heaven,
      sing without ceasing.

2 Their hymn is ever: "Holy, holy, holy,
   Lord God almighty, heaven and earth give glory."
   Apostles, prophets, martyrs throng to praise you,
      joined by the whole Church.

3 Praise to the Father, of unbounded glory,
   and only true Son, worthy of all worship,
   and Holy Spirit, source of truth and comfort:
      God in three Persons.

4 Christ, king of glory, only Son eternal,
   you took our nature, from the Virgin's womb borne,
   and brought us freedom, overcoming death's sting,
      unbarring heaven.

5 Now high exalted, you will come to judge us.
   Lord, help your people, bought by your own life's blood;
   bring us to glory, that with saints and angels,
      there we may praise you.

—Carl P. Daw, Jr.

This ancient Christian hymn is appointed for use at the Order of Worship for Evening and at Evening Prayer (BCP, pp. 64, 112, 118).

TUNE: This text was written specifically for the tune ST. CLEMENT.

1 "Thrills and gladdens" is an attempt to capture the Greek *hilaron* (from which comes the English "exhilarating").

2 The second line of this stanza recalls the origins of this hymn in domestic lamp-lighting ceremonies in Christian homes (after the model of Jewish domestic worship). In lieu of the traditional Trinitarian language, the final line of this stanza may be sung as "to praise the true and living God."

3 If it is desired to avoid the male language of the third line, the first half may be sung as "Incarnate God."

O LIGHT WHOSE SPLENDOR THRILLS AND GLADDENS

9 8. 9 8.

1 O Light whose splendor thrills and gladdens
    with radiance brighter than the sun,
pure gleam of God's unending glory,
    O Jesus, blest Anointed One;

2 as twilight hovers near at sunset,
    and lamps are lit, and children nod,
in evening hymns we lift our voices
    to Father, Spirit, Son: one God.

3 In all life's brilliant, timeless moments,
    let faithful voices sing your praise,
O Son of God, our Life-bestower,
    whose glory lightens endless days.

—3rd century Greek hymn;
para. Carl P. Daw, Jr.

CHRISTIAN
MINISTRY

This text represents two layers of revision to the original version by Denis Wortman. The Text Committee for *The Hymnal 1982* made revisions (which were in turn amended by the 1982 General Convention) to make the human references inclusive (stanza 1), to improve singability (stanza 2), and to present a sounder doctrine of priesthood (stanza 3). The process has been admirably continued by the compilers of *The Psalter Hymnal* (1987), who turned third-person references to first-person and "thee/thou" language to "you."

TUNE: The customary tune is TOULON.

1 Wortman's text originally read "prophets' sons," which made the hymn unusable at the ordination of women. The biblical imagery comes from 2 Kings 2:1-15.

2 The second through fourth stanzas deal with the three kinds of anointed persons: prophets, priests, and kings. Cf. the text in this collection, "Let kings and prophets yield their name" (p. 139).

3 This stanza combines language of 1 Peter 2:4-9 ("royal priesthood"/"living sacrifice") and the Eucharistic prayer ("our sacrifice of praise and thanksgiving" BCP, p. 335).

4 The latter half of the first line of the fourth stanza is one of the most significant improvements made by the *Psalter Hymnal* revision. Cf. Revelation 5:10, which is paraphrased in the hymn "Splendor and honor, majesty and power" (p. 115).

God of the Prophets,
Bless the Prophets' Heirs!

10 10. 10 10

1 God of the prophets, bless the prophets' heirs!
    Elijah's mantle o'er Elisha cast:
each age for your own solemn task prepares;
    make each one stronger, nobler than the last.

2 Anoint us prophets! Teach us your intent:
    to human need our quickened hearts awake:
fill us with power, our lips make eloquent
    for righteousness that shall all evil break.

3 Anoint us priests! Help us to intercede
    with all your royal priesthood born of grace:
though us your church presents in word and deed
    a living sacrifice of thanks and praise.

4 Anoint us kings! Help us do justice, Lord!
    Anoint us with the Spirit of your Son:
ours not a monarch's crown or tyrant's sword;
    ours by the love of Christ a kingdom won.

5 Make us apostles, heralds of your cross;
    forth may we go to tell all realms your grace:
by you inspired may we count all but loss,
    and stand at last with joy before your face.

stanzas 1,2,4,5, Denis Wortman, alt:
stanza 3, Carl P. Daw, Jr., rev.

This hymn was written as a gift to Jeffery Rowthorn for his consecration as Bishop Suffragan of the Diocese of Connecticut on September 19, 1987, when it was sung for the first time.

TUNE: At its first use, the text was sung to the tune JEFFERSON because the publishing history of that tune has connections with New Haven, where the consecration took place. It has since appeared with HYFRYDOL in several hymnals and works well with tunes which have an effective turn at the midpoint (e.g. IN BABILONE, NETTLETON).

1 The first stanza is addressed to the Third Person of the Trinity rather than the First because the traditional prayers and hymns of the ordination rites (especially "Veni Creator Spiritus" and "Veni Sancte Spiritus") are so addressed. "Guide and guardian" is an attempt to paraphrase the Greek term *Paraklete* (John 14:26); "wind-sped flame" recalls the first Christian Pentecost (Acts 2:1-4); "hovering dove" alludes to the Baptism of Christ (Matthew 3:13-17; Mark 1:9-11; Luke 3:21-22; John 1:32-33); "breath of life" refers to creation (Genesis 2:7); "voice of prophets" echoes the Nicene Creed, which is part of the consecration rite (BCP, p. 520); "sign of blessing" refers to the gift of the Holy Spirit at Baptism (BCP, p. 308); "power of love" pulls together Jesus' words to the disciples (Acts 1:8) and the well-known hymn "Come down, O Love divine." The petition employs language from the actual consecration prayer invoking the Spirit "with whom [Christ] endowed the apostles, and by whom your Church is built up in every place" (BCP, p. 521).

2 The attributes of the Second Person of the Trinity are perhaps more familiar and require less explanation. The central image is Christ as the Good Shepherd (John 10:11-16), which is frequently invoked in the consecration rite. For example, the bishop-elect promises to carry out pastoral responsibilities "in the name of Christ, the Shepherd and Bishop of our souls" (BCP, p. 518: an echo of 1 Peter 2:25). The present reading of the fifth line ("all pastors") calls attention to the root meaning of that term, but the original reading was "all bishops." (In various hymnals permission has been given to alter this line further as needed for special situations.)

3 In the stanza directed to the First Person of the Trinity, the epithets are attempts to recast traditional understandings in gender-free language. "Life-bestower," though used in the *Phos hilaron* as an attribute of Christ (BCP, pp. 64, 112, 118; cf. the paraphrase in this collection at p. 121) and in the Nicene Creed as an attribute of the Holy Spirit (BCP, pp. 327, 359), represents a significant aspect of what was once intended by calling the First Person our Father, since it was assumed until

(continued on p. 128)

GOD THE SPIRIT, GUIDE AND GUARDIAN

87.87.D

1 God the Spirit, guide and guardian,
    wind-sped flame and hovering dove,
breath of life and voice of prophets,
    sign of blessing, power of love:
give to those who lead your people
    fresh anointing of your grace;
send them forth as bold apostles
    to your Church in every place.

2 Christ our Savior, Sovereign, Shepherd,
    Word-made-flesh, Love crucified,
teacher, healer, suffering Servant,
    friend of sinners, foe of pride:
in your tending may all pastors
    learn and live a Shepherd's care;
grant them courage and compassion
    shown through word and deed and prayer.

3 Great Creator, Life-bestower,
    Truth beyond all thought's recall,
fount of wisdom, womb of mercy,
    giving and forgiving all:
as you know our strength and weakness,
    so may those the Church exalts
oversee her life steadfastly
    yet not overlook her faults.

4 Triune God, mysterious Being,
    undivided and diverse,
deeper than our minds can fathom,
    greater than our creeds rehearse:
help us in our varied callings
    your full image to proclaim,
that our ministries uniting
    may give glory to your Name.

—Carl P. Daw, Jr.

This hymn was written for Arthur Willis, for the celebration of the fiftieth anniversary of his ordination held on 29 September 1987.

TUNE: The text fits a number of majestic tunes in this metre (e.g. AUSTRIA, TON-Y-BOTEL, IN BABILONE), but it works best with Beethoven's HYMN TO JOY (especially in a version that preserves the syncopation which falls on the word "joins").

1 This text draws heavily on the opening clause of the Collect for the feast of St. Michael and All Angels: "Everlasting God, you have ordained and constituted in a wonderful order the ministries of angels and mortals" (BCP, p. 244). "Messenger" is the literal meaning of the Greek word *angelos*. The second line recalls Luke 2:8-14, and the fourth is intended to echo appointed readings for the day (Genesis 28:12 and John 1:51). To suggest that the ministry of angels and mortals is joined as indissolubly as the divinity and humanity of Christ may at first appear rash, but further reflection seems to justify such an assertion.

2 The second stanza focuses on the ministry of mortals (and not necessarily ordained ones!). The third line attempts to capture how the setting apart of any person for a special ministry is a challenge to all Christians to offer their lives for God's service. The conventional identification of heaven as "above" needs to be understood as metaphorical shorthand for "beyond human experience or comprehension" rather than as a literal location. The last two lines are intended to recall Revelation 5:11-12, which is part of one of the appointed lessons at Evening Prayer on this day.

---

continued notes for "God the Spirit, Guide and Guardian"

the nineteenth century that the male provided all the life-bearing substance needed for procreation. "Womb of mercy" reflects the fact that the Hebrew and Aramaic words for mercy are derived from a root meaning "womb." "Giving and forgiving" is shamelessly lifted from the third stanza of Henry Van Dyke's hymn "Joyful, joyful, we adore thee." The oversee/overlook pun of the last two lines is a play on the Greek word for bishop, *episkopos* (literally "overseer"). The feminine pronoun is used for the Church as the Bride of Christ (Revelation 21:2).

4 As the first three stanzas have invoked the special attributes of the three Persons of the Trinity to aid the person(s) being ordained, so the final stanza calls on the undivided Trinity to bless the full range of ministries entrusted to the Church. The diversity of lay and ordained ministries is a reflection of the plenitude of God, yet even the sum of them falls far short of God's full glory.

MESSENGERS OF GOD'S OWN SENDING

87.87.D

1 Messengers of God's own sending,
    heralds of the Savior's birth,
  emblems of the life unending,
    spirits binding heav'n and earth:
  so the ministry of angels
    (like our Lord's divinity)
  joins the ministry of mortals
    serving long and faithfully.

2 Messengers of God's salvation,
    heralds of the Savior's love,
  emblems of our life's oblation,
    pilgrims bound for heav'n above:
  so the ministry of mortals
    (like our Lord's humanity)
  joins the ministry of angels
    praising God eternally.

—Carl P. Daw, Jr.

THE LIFE
OF FAITH

This is a revised form of a paraphrase of Psalm 19 originally written for Alec Wyton and included in his musical work "Sing a New Song unto the Lord" commissioned by the General Synod of the Associate Reformed Presbyterian Church for its Bicentennial Anniversary in 1982. The text was revised in 1988 for publication in *Psalms for Today*.

TUNE: This text works well with ST. PATRICK'S BREASTPLATE.

1 The three stanzas of this hymn reflect the three parts of Psalm 19. The first section focuses on the revelation of God through creation.

2 The second section celebrates the revelation of God's love through the giving of the Law.

3 The final part of the psalm is the human response to these two revelations of God's power and care.

God's Glory Fills the Heavens with Hymns

LMD

1 God's glory fills the heavens with hymns,
  the domed sky bears the Maker's mark;
new praises sound from day to day
  and echo through the knowing dark.
Without a word their songs roll on,
  into all lands their voices run.
And with a champion's strength and grace
  from farthest heaven comes forth the sun.

2 God's perfect law revives the soul;
  its precepts make the simple wise;
its just commands rejoice the heart;
  its truth gives light unto the eyes.
For ever shall this law endure:
  unblemished, righteous, true, complete.
No gold was ever found so fine,
  no honey in the comb more sweet.

3 God's servant may I ever be:
  this world my joy, that word my guide.
O cleanse me, Lord, from secret sin:
  deliver me from selfish pride.
Accept my thoughts and words and deeds:
  let them find favor in your sight.
For you alone can make me whole,
  O Lord, my refuge and my might.

—Carl P. Daw, Jr.

This text was commissioned by St. Andrew's Episcopal Church in Amarillo, Texas, for the midyear conference of the Region VII members of the Association of Anglican Musicians in January 1986. It was originally performed in an anthem setting by David Ashley White.

TUNE: This text was written to be sung to BROTHER JAMES AIR.

1 People who are uncomfortable with "Lord" in the opening line may sing "My God and Shepherd." It is worth noting that the passive constructions in this hymn reflect a conscious effort to reclaim the "theological passive" which implies divine action, since God is the ultimate source of all activity.

2 Even today in Israel shepherds must often lead their flocks to streams which flow between cave-riddled cliffs, where in ancient times bands of robbers frequently hid. These areas were so treacherous that even the Roman army pursued only the most desperate criminals that far. Because these water-worn valleys are usually deep and narrow, they are in shadow most of the time. In effect, the pastoral images of nourishment in the midst of danger are anticipations of the feast in the presence of enemies.

3 Anointing oneself with scented olive oil or other perfumed ointments was part of daily grooming for the rich in the ancient Near East (cf. Ruth 3:3). It was therefore a sign of favor towards an honored guest (Luke 7:46). Ointments, oils, and unguents were also prized for their cooling and pain-relieving effect in a hot and dry climate, and they were frequently used as part of medical treatment (Isaiah 1:6; Luke 10:34).

4 God's faithful covenant love (*hesed;* RSV "steadfast love") is experienced most powerfully in the context of Temple worship.

THE LORD MY SHEPHERD GUARDS ME WELL

8 6. 8 6. 4 4. 6

1 The Lord my Shepherd guards me well,
    and all my wants are fed:
amid green pastures made to lie,
    beside still waters led.
My careworn soul
grows strong and whole
    when God's true path I tread.

2 Though I should walk in darkest ways
    through valleys like the grave,
no evil shall I ever fear;
    your presence makes me brave.
On my behalf
your rod and staff
    assure me you will save.

3 For me a table has been spread
    where all my foes can see;
you bathe my head with fragrant oil
    to soothe and honor me.
My heart and cup
are both filled up
    with joyful ecstasy.

4 Your steadfast love will follow me
    to shield me all my days
and bring me to your holy house,
    redeemed from error's ways,
my whole life long
to join the song
    of those who sing God's praise.

—Carl P. Daw, Jr.

TUNE: A number of Common Metre tunes work well with this text, especially GEORGETOWN, BANGOR, MARTYRDOM, and NEW BRITAIN.

1 The first stanza is a reflection on John 14:2.

2 This stanza is both an affirmation that God's activity is not limited to the received body of Christian belief and an encouragement to recognize where and how God is at work in ways we do not anticipate (or perhaps even like).

3 The third stanza weaves together allusions to John 8:82, 14:5 and a phrase ("whose service is perfect freedom") from the Collect for Peace (BCP, p. 57 [cf. p. 69]).

4 The late Urban T. Holmes III used to define *metanoia* or conversion as "God's gift of room to turn around in" (cf. *Turning to Christ: A Theology of Renewal and Evangelization* [New York: Seabury Press, 1981], p. 8). The final line is a recollection of Psalm 42:2 (see "As panting deer desire the waterbrooks," p. 61).

THE HOUSE OF FAITH HAS MANY ROOMS

C.M.

1 The house of faith has many rooms
    where we have never been;
  there is more space within God's scope
    than we have ever seen.

2 We dare not limit God's domain
    to what our creeds declare,
  or shrink from probing things unknown
    lest God should not be there,

3 The way to God is not escape,
    though truth does make us free:
  the life of chosen servanthood
    is perfect liberty.

4 Yet still we seek at journey's end
    the last and sweetest grace:
  the gift of room to turn around
    and know God face to face.

—Carl P. Daw, Jr.

This text was commissioned by St. Andrew's Episcopal Church, Amarillo, Texas, to be set as an anthem by David Ashley White for the Region VII midwinter meeting of the Association of Anglican Musicians on the eve of the feast of the Confession of Peter (January 18) in 1986.

TUNE: Of the available hymn tunes in the appropriate metre, the most effective with this text is probably MELITA.

1 Though both the kings and prophets of Israel were anointed as a sign of God's favor and blessing on them, the true Messiah/Christ is Jesus. (*Christos* is the Greek equivalent of the Hebrew *mashiah;* both terms mean "anointed one.")

2 Recent discussions of faith development by James Fowler, John Westerhoff, and others have identified "searching faith"—an attitude of probing the limits of what one believes—as an integral part of a person's spiritual growth. For other hymns celebrating this often-neglected aspect of faith, see "Praise God whose providential awkwardness" (p. 97) and "When Thomas heard the strange report" (p. 79). For the biblical account of this episode see Matthew 16:13-20 (also Mark 8:27-30 and Luke 9:18-22), the appointed Gospel for this feast.

3 The third stanza incorporates allusions to the other scriptures appointed for the day, which describe Peter's preaching (Acts 4:8-13) and recall Peter's traditional role as a bishop and shepherd of souls (John 21:15-17; 1 Peter 5:14) in imitation of the Good Shepherd (Psalm 23).

LET KINGS AND PROPHETS YIELD THEIR NAME

8 8. 8 8. 8 8

1 Let kings and prophets yield their name
    to Jesus, true Anointed One,
for whom a nation looked in hope
    yet failed to see that God had done
a strange and unexpected thing:
God sent a servant, not a king.

2 But God reveals to searching faith
    the truths that pious dogmas hide:
when Jesus asked the twelve his name,
    blunt Peter stepped forth and replied
in words that seemed both right and odd:
"You are Messiah, Son of God."

3 Give us, O God, the grace to know
    the limits of our certainty:
help us, like Peter, to declare
    the still-unfolding mystery
of One who reigns though sacrificed,
our Lamb and Shepherd, Jesus Christ.

—Carl P. Daw, Jr.

Although Psalm 137 is never appointed for use in the Eucharistic lectionary, it is one of the most beautiful and haunting of all the psalms.

TUNE: With minor adaptation, the tune of the spiritual GO DOWN, MOSES can be used with these words. The resulting combination is especially poignant because it links the Egyptian and Babylonian exiles. In performance, the first and third lines of each stanza could be sung by cantor or choir, with the congregation responding with the second and fourth lines of the stanza and all joining in the refrain.

1-4 The stanzas paraphrase Psalm 137:1-3, 5-6; the refrain is based on Psalm 137:4.

'

Beside the Streams of Babylon

C.M. with Refrain

1 Beside the streams of Babylon,
    we sat down and we wept:
when Zion's memory came to mind,
    we sat down and we wept.

    REFRAIN: *God's song, God's song,*
        how shall we sing God's song,
        God's song, God's song,
        in a faraway land?

2 We could not bear to play our harps,
    we hung them on the trees;
there in that bitter distant land,
    we hung them on the trees.
    REFRAIN

3 Our captors asked us for a song,
    "A song of Zion, sing!"
And our oppressors called for mirth,
    "A song of Zion, sing!"
    REFRAIN

4 My right hand may forget its skill
    but not Jerusalem:
my tongue forget to speak again,
    but not Jerusalem.
    REFRAIN

—Carl P. Daw, Jr.

This text was commissioned by St. Andrew's Episcopal Church in Amarillo. Texas.

TUNE: This text was written to be used with the tune ABBOT'S LEIGH.

1   The first stanza is drawn from John 1:35-41.

2   The calling of Andrew is described in Matthew 4:18-19/Mark 1:16-18. The various events mentioned in the latter part of this stanza are recorded in John 6:8-9, John 12:20-22, and Acts 1:13, 2:1-4.

3   The first half of this stanza recalls that by tradition Andrew was martyred on a saltire (X-shaped) cross, which has become his emblem in Christian art. The concluding sentence is based on the Collect for St. Andrew's Day (November 30), which includes a petition that we may "bring those near to us into [Christ's] gracious presence" (BCP, p. 237).

SING OF ANDREW, JOHN'S DISCIPLE

87.87. D

1 Sing of Andrew, John's disciple,
    led by faith through ways untrod,
till the Baptist cried at Jordan,
    "There behold the Lamb of God."
Stirred by hearing this new teacher,
    Andrew, freed from doubt and fear,
ran to tell his brother Simon,
    "God's Anointed One is here!"

2 Sing of Andrew, called by Jesus
    from the shores of Galilee,
leaving boats and nets and kindred,
    trusting in that "Follow me."
When a lad's small meal fed thousands,
    when inquiring Greeks found care,
when the Spirit came in blessing,
    Andrew faithfully was there.

3 Sing of Andrew, bold apostle,
    sent to make the gospel known,
faithful to his Lord's example,
    called to make a cross his own.
So may we who prize his memory
    honor Christ in our own day,
bearing witness to our neighbors,
    living what we sing and pray.

—Carl P. Daw, Jr.

This hymn is a paraphrase of the Nunc dimittis or Song of Simeon (Luke 2:29-32), which is occasionally sung as a canticle at Morning Prayer (BCP, pp. 51. 93) and is regularly sung at Evening Prayer and Compline (BCP, pp. 66, 120, 135).

TUNE: This text was written specifically for Gibbons' SONG 1.

1 Lines three and four attempt to convey the double sense of salvation personified which is inherent in the original idiom. In the infant Jesus, Simeon sees the fulfillment of Israel's call to be a light to the nations (Isaiah 42:6, 49:6).

NOW HAVE YOU SET YOUR SERVANT FREE, O LORD

10 10. 10 10. 10 10.

Now have you set your servant free, O Lord,
to go in peace according to your word.
For I have seen your promised victory
in One prepared for all the world to see:
a Light for nations who in darkness dwell,
the glory of your people Israel.

—Carl P. Daw, Jr.

This hymn is a paraphrase of Canticle 9: The First Song of Isaiah (Isaiah 12:2-6), which is appointed for use at Morning Prayer (BCP, p. 86). It was written for *The Hymnal 1982* and has been set as an anthem by David Ashley White (Augsburg 11-2357).

TUNE: This text appears in *The Hymnal 1982* with two tunes, COLLEGE OF PREACHERS and THOMAS MERTON. It may also be sung effectively to IN BABILONE or NETTLETON.

1 The opening line of the hymn is identical to that of the Prayer Book canticle. For this edition the second line has been revised to eliminate the male pronoun for God, since it does not occur at that point in the Hebrew text.

2 For this edition the pronoun "his" has been replaced with "God's" in the first and fourth lines of this stanza. The second line is an intentional echo of Timothy Dudley-Smith's metrical paraphrase based on the New English Bible's translation of the Magnificat, "Tell out, my soul, the greatness of the Lord."

SURELY IT IS GOD WHO SAVES ME

8 7. 8 7. D

1 Surely it is God who saves me;
 I shall trust and have no fear.
For the Lord defends and shields me
 and his saving help is near.
So rejoice as you draw water
 from salvation's healing spring;
in the day of your deliverance
 thank the Lord, his mercies sing.

2 Make God's deeds known to the peoples:
 tell out his exalted Name.
Praise the Lord, who has done great things;
 all his works God's might proclaim.
Zion, lift your voice in singing;
 for with you has come to dwell,
in your very midst the great and
 Holy One of Israel.

—Carl P. Daw, Jr.

This hymn is a paraphrase of the Kontakion for the Departed from the Eastern Orthodox Memorial Service as it appears in the Order for Burial in the Book of Common Prayer (pp. 483, 499).

TUNE: This paraphrase was written specifically for the tune RUSSIA in order to preserve some of the flavor of the original text for congregations unable to sing the traditional Kiev melody for the Kontakion.

1 The addition of the epithet "Victorious" is an intentional allusion to the Christus Victor view of atonement, most notably set forth by Gustav Aulen in his book of that title (London: S.P.C.K., 1931). "Regions of light" echoes the traditional exchange at prayers for the departed: "Rest eternal grant to them, O Lord." "And let light perpetual shine upon them" (cf. BCP, pp. 387, 486, 502).

2 In the second stanza the mystery of humanity's creation in the image of God (Genesis 1:26-27) is recalled by the expansion of the Kontakion text to include the adjective "glorious."

3 The second line of the third stanza quotes God's words to Adam (Genesis 3:19), which are also used on Ash Wednesday at the Imposition of Ashes (BCP, p. 265). This language is further employed in the Burial Office in the well-known words of the Commendatory Prayer: "ashes to ashes, dust to dust" (BCP, pp. 485, 501). "Alleluia" derives from the Hebrew "Hallelujah," which is usually rendered in English as "Praise the Lord!" Its celebratory character is so strong that it is completely omitted from the liturgy during Lent. (Please note: The preferred way of dealing with the lack of one syllable in this final line of the third stanza is to sing two notes on the second syllable of the first "Alleluia.")

CHRIST THE VICTORIOUS, GIVE TO YOUR SERVANTS

11 10. 11 10

1 Christ the Victorious, give to your servants
rest with your saints in the regions of light.
Grief and pain ended, and sighing no longer,
there may they find everlasting life.

2 Only Immortal One, Mighty Creator!
We are your creatures and children of earth.
From earth you formed us, both glorious and mortal,
and to the earth shall we all return.

3 God-spoken prophecy, word at creation:
"You came from dust and to dust shall return."
Yet at the grave shall we raise up our glad song,
"Alleluia, alleluia!"

4 Christ the Victorious, give to your servants
rest with your saints in the regions of light.
Grief and pain ended, and sighing no longer,
there may they find everlasting life.

—Carl P. Daw, Jr.

HYMNS FOR DAILY LIFE

TUNE: This text is intended for use with Erik Routley's tune SHARPTHORNE.

1 The immediate stimulus for writing this hymn was the rather depressing experience of reading through a number of hymnals, all of which seemed predicated on the assumption that God is glorified by deprecating human beings. The first stanza especially recalls Genesis 1:26-28a.

2 This stanza is, in part, a condensed form of the hymn "Ubi caritas et amor" translated in full at p. 69. It is an affirmation that God's love is capable of working even when we do not acknowledge it or consciously invoke it. All love, however fragmented or inadequate, ultimately derives from God's love for all creation.

3 It was once asserted that God was completely immovable and could not feel pain, but that dogma has yielded in recent times to an appreciation of God's compassionate identification with all who suffer and all who are outcast.

4 The Incarnate Love of God revealed in Jesus Christ is not an anomaly but the palpable expression of the abiding faithfulness of God. The self-giving of the Trinity in creation is recalled and made present (*anamnesis*) in the redemptive work of Christ's death, resurrection, and ascension.

God Is Not Lifted Up

66.66.33.6

1 God is not lifted up
   by bringing people down;
   for the Creator's heart
   is through creation known:
   > God's image
   > and likeness
   > take flesh in human life.

2 God's presence is revealed
   through caring words and deeds,
   when people live in peace
   and share each other's needs:
   > God's mercy
   > and goodness
   > take flesh in human love.

3 God does not stand apart
   from frailty or distress
   but yearns to soothe our griefs
   and heal our brokenness:
   > God's longing
   > and suffering
   > take flesh in human pain.

4 God's servant-love has joined
   our human history
   through One who died and rose
   to make us whole and free:
   > God's perfect
   > self-offering
   > took flesh in Jesus Christ.

—Carl P. Daw, Jr.

This text was written at the request of Alec Wyton for a text on labor which could be used with his tune COBURN and has been published with it in an anthem setting (H.W.Gray GOMR 3484).

TUNE: In addition to the tune for which it was written, this text can also be sung effectively to LOMBARD STREET (*The Hymnal 1940*).

1 The identification of Jesus as a Carpenter (Mark 6:3) is probably derived from the occupation of his guardian Joseph (Matthew 13:55). The last two lines of this stanza call attention to the importance of understanding that the pre-incarnate Christ was engaged in the work of creation (John 1:1-3).

2 The primary scripture references here are Genesis 3:19 and John 1:14.

3 Much of the language here is derived from the collects "for Vocation in Daily Work" and "For Labor Day" (BCP p. 261).

4 The first two lines of this stanza are based on Matthew 11:28-30. In traditional theological categories, the "work of Christ" is the label given to discussions of atonement.

WHAT BOUNDLESS LOVE,
O CARPENTER OF NAZARETH

12. 10. 12. 10

1 What boundless love, O Carpenter of Nazareth,
    brought you to earth to share our human toil?
Was there no task in heaven's vast infinity
    fit for the hands that formed us from the soil?

2 Could Adam's fate, to earn his bread by sweat of brow,
    be turned to blessing or less bitter made?
Yet for our sake the Word took flesh and sanctified
    our daily labor by his humble trade.

3 Still in our midst, this Lord of shop and marketplace
    prays through our work of body, mind, and strength,
and calls us all to labor for the common good,
    led by his love that knows no breadth or length.

4 O come to him, you laborers who long for rest; his yoke
    is easy and his burden light.
That mighty work he did for you on Calvary forever
    gives you favor in God's sight.

—Carl P. Daw, Jr.

This hymn was written at the suggestion of Jeffery Rowthorn for consideration for a hymnal for colleges and universities.

TUNE: This text was specifically written for Holst's tune THAXTED, for which my wife and other friends had asked me to provide new words. That tune seems especially appropriate, not only because of its grandeur, but also because it is not associated with any particular religious tradition.

1 The first stanza deals with broad categories of study such as the natural sciences, the arts, and the humanities, as well as with the task of describing and explaining the results of such study.

2 The second stanza approaches the experience of education in terms of the people involved: scholars, teachers, students, as well as the support staff and the unseen donors who are an essential part of maintaining institutions of higher education.

FOR THE SPLENDOR OF CREATION

86.86.87.86.86.86

1 For the splendor of creation
   that draws us to inquire,
for the mysteries of knowledge
   to which our hearts aspire,
for the deep and subtle beauties
   which delight the eye and ear,
for the discipline of logic,
   the struggle to be clear,
for the unexplained remainder,
   the puzzling and the odd:
for the joy and pain of learning,
   we give you thanks, O God.

2 For the scholars past and present
   whose bounty we digest,
for the teachers who inspire us
   to summon forth our best,
for our rivals and companions,
   sometimes foolish, sometimes wise,
for the human web upholding
   this noble enterprise,
for the common life that binds us
   through days that soar or plod:
for this place and for these people,
   we give you thanks, O God.

—Carl P. Daw, Jr.

FROM WORSHIP
TO WITNESS

This hymn was commissioned as part of the Tricentennial celebration of Eastern Shore Chapel (Episcopal), Virginia Beach, Virginia, commemorating its founding in 1689. The motto for the celebration was "Repeat the sounding joy," which the committee hoped to have incorporated into the text.

TUNE: No tune is suggested here because one was to be commissioned. David Hurd has written the tune EASTERN SHORE CHAPEL for this text. Other tunes that would work well include HOLY MANNA, RAQUEL, and IN BABILONE.

1 The first stanza calls attention to the two interrelated parts of the Eucharist, Word and Table, by intentionally mixing the language associated with each part. This reflects not merely a poetic license but a deep conviction that we are fed through hearing God's Word read and preached and that we proclaim the Good News by sharing the consecrated Bread and Wine.

2 This stanza is largely derived from the post-communion prayers of the Eucharist (BCP, pp. 365-366). The third and fourth lines are a reworking of the Dismissal: "Go in peace to love and serve the Lord" (BCP, p. 366). For other explorations of the image of God/Christ in humanity, see the hymns "God is not lifted up" (p. 153) and "Gentle Joseph heard a warning" (p. 39).

3 Much of the language here is derived from the Parable of the Banquet (Matthew 22:1-10: Luke 14:16-24). The final line, as noted above, was the motto for the parish's celebration: it comes from the second stanza of Isaac Watts' great Christmas hymn, "Joy to the World."

As We Gather at Your Table

87.87.D

1 As we gather at your Table,
  as we listen to your Word,
help us know, O God, your presence:
  let our hearts and minds be stirred.
Nourish us with sacred story
  till we claim it as our own;
teach us through this holy banquet
  how to make Love's victory known.

2 Turn our worship into witness
  in the sacrament of life;
send us forth to love and serve you,
  bringing peace where there is strife.
Give us, Christ, your great compassion
  to forgive as you forgave;
may we still behold your image
  in the world you died to save.

3 Gracious Spirit, help us summon
  other guests to share that feast
where triumphant Love will welcome
  those who had been last and least.
There no more will envy blind us
  nor will pride our peace destroy,
as we join with saints and angels
  to repeat the sounding joy.

—Carl P. Daw, Jr.

This hymn grew out of a suggestion by Charles Price that the raising of Lazarus would be a good image around which to develop a hymn on healing.

TUNE: This text was written with the tune BANGOR in mind.

1 The story is told in John 11:1-44.

2 The true ministry of healing is not something that can be undertaken lightly or dispassionately. It is a costly and sacred gift which should not be abused.

3 To those who have been entrusted with the gift of healing, the greatest temptation is the spiritual pride of believing oneself to be indispensable to God's purposes. There is also a danger of attempting to divorce religious involvement from the totality of one's life.

4 See Romans 12:2 and John 10:10.

5 We are enabled to share God's love not so much by our woundedness (*pace* Henri Nouwen) as by our experience of having been healed and of living in a continual process of being healed.

"COME, LAZARUS," THE SAVIOR CALLED

CM

1 "Come, Lazarus," the Savior called;
  and from the stony grave
came forth his friend, from death unthralled,
  to show God's power to save.

2 It was no light or easy task
  to wake this one who slept;
the Healer feigned no callous mask:
  moved deeply, Jesus wept.

3 Fill us with your compassion, Lord,
  our fear and pride remove,
till all our lives enflesh your word
  and bear your wounds of love.

4 Convert our wills and make us whole;
  wean us from selfish strife;
transform each heart and mind and soul
  with your abundant life.

5 Then send us forth to show your love
  in every time and place,
that healed and healing, we may prove
  the channels of your grace.

—Carl P. Daw, Jr.

This hymn was written in 1985 as part of an invited competition for a hymn to commemorate the Centennial of the Women's Missionary Union of the Southern Baptist Convention, and this text was the winner of that competition.

TUNE: Once the text had been chosen, there was a contest for a tune. The tune chosen was NALL AVENUE by A.L. Butler, and it was widely circulated throughout the Southern Baptist Convention. The text can also be sung to a number of other tunes in this metre, such as PLEADING SAVIOR or IN BABILONE.

1 God is appropriately called our Author because creation resulted from the utterance of God's spoken word (Genesis 1:1-2:3). The first two lines also draw on Paul's sermon in Athens (Acts 17:22-31). The guidelines for the competition specifically asked that there be attention to carrying out mission in daily life, and all three stanzas of the hymn include the word "lives." This text also tries to avoid the implied tone of superiority which is characteristic of many nineteenth-century mission hymns.

2 As the creativity of God offers a motive for feeling related to all people, so God's incarnation in Jesus Christ offers an example of perseverance and patience. In the tradition of those who were first sent out (i.e. the apostles), we seek Christ's strength and guidance. The final line paraphrases Romans 12:2.

3 The sustaining and inspiring power of God is made known through the work of the Holy Spirit. The succinct expression of the gospel message in line four is intended to recall John 3:16-17.

GOD OUR AUTHOR AND CREATOR

8.7.8.7.D

1   God our Author and Creator,
      in whose life we find our own,
  make our daily witness greater,
      by our lives make your love known.
  Help us show how love embraces
      those whom fear and greed downtrod;
  in all yearning hearts and faces
      let us see a child of God.

2   Like those first apostles, Savior,
      give us strength to love and serve:
  when our fainting spirits waver,
      fire our hearts and steel our nerve.
  Teach us wisdom and compassion:
      bid our restless thoughts be still;
  by your guidance help us fashion
      lives conformed unto your will.

3   Keep us faithful, Holy Spirit,
      help us bear the message true,
  that at last all lands may hear it:
      "God is love; Christ died for you."
  Join our lives in mighty chorus
      till we come from every place,
  with all those who went before us,
      to the fullness of God's grace.

—Carl P. Daw, Jr.

This hymn was written at the request of the Text Committee for *The Hymnal 1982* in response to several requests for a new hymn on peace.

TUNE: This text was written specifically for Parry's JERUSALEM. Anthem settings of that tune with these words have been prepared by Alec Wyton (Sacred Music Press S-318) and Richard Proulx (GIA G-2689).

1 This hymn deals with two aspects of peace: *pax*, an understanding of peace based on the cessation of conflict, and *shalom*, the condition of living abundantly in harmony and mutual goodwill. The former approach informs the first stanza, and the latter the second stanza. Although this hymn affirms that peace is always God's gift, it also recognizes the importance of human responsibility in preparing an environment in which peace can flourish.

2 This stanza is a paraphrase of Isaiah 11:6-9. It was, in fact, written before the first stanza. Structurally, it describes the peaceful existence for which the first stanza prays.